PISODE ONE

1. **PROLOGUE/TITLES.**

2. **CLEARING ON THE MOUNTAINSIDE. NIGHT.**

    IT IS A DARK AND STORMY NIGHT. SOMEWHERE IN A CLEARING IN A FOREST IN THE RAMTOP MOUNTAINS, THREE WITCHES, MAGRAT GARLICK, GRANNY WEATHERWAX AND NANNY OGG, ARE GATHERED.

    MAGRAT: Ha Ha Ha. When shall we three meet again?!?

    THERE IS A DEAFENING CRACK OF THUNDER AND LIGHTNING AS THE SKY CRACKS OPEN.

    GRANNY W.: Well, I can do next Tuesday.

3. **LANCRE CASTLE. NIGHT.**

    VERENCE: *(O.O.S.)* Aaaaarghhhhh!!!

    KING VERENCE, A DAGGER BETWEEN HIS SHOULDER-BLADES, IS TUMBLING DOWN THE STAIRS.

4. **LANCRE CASTLE. COURTYARD. NIGHT.**

    COACH DRIVER: Ha! Get up.

    A HORSE PULLS A REGAL-LOOKING COACH THROUGH THE GATEWAY AND OVER THE DRAWBRIDGE OF THE CASTLE.

5. **LANCRE CASTLE. NIGHT.**

    AS VERENCE CONTINUES TO TUMBLE DOWN THE STAIRS, THE SHADOWY FIGURE OF DUKE FELMET CAN BE SEEN BRIEFLY IN ONE OF THE ARCHES LOOKING WITH SATISFACTION AT THE FALLING BODY. THERE IS BLOOD ON HIS HANDS, WHICH HE TRIES TO WIPE OFF.

6. **FOREST. NIGHT.**

    COACH DRIVER: Ha!

    THE COACH RATTLES PAST AT A TERRIFIC RATE.

7. **LANCRE CASTLE. NIGHT.**

    VERENCE: Aaagh.

    VERENCE COMES TO REST AT THE FOOT OF THE STAIRS, THE DAGGER IN HIS BACK. A SHADOWY FIGURE CAN BE SEEN MOVING NEARBY.

8. **CLEARING ON THE MOUNTAINSIDE. NIGHT.**

    GRANNY W.: Tuesday all right for you, Gytha?

    NANNY O.: What for?

    MAGRAT: To be abroad.

TERRY PRATCHETT'S
Discworld
WYRD SISTERS

THE ILLUSTRATED SCREENPLAY

CORGI BOOKS

WYRD SISTERS: THE ILLUSTRATED SCREENPLAY
A CORGI BOOK : 0 552 14575 0

First publication in Great Britain

PRINTING HISTORY
Corgi edition published 1998

Set in Metro and Blur by Production Line, Minster Lovell, Oxford

Corgi Books are published by Transworld Publishers Ltd,
61-63 Uxbridge Road, London W5 5SA
in Australia by Transworld Publishers (Australia) Pty Ltd,
15-25 Helles Avenue, Moorebank, NSW 2170
and in New Zealand by Transworld Publishers (NZ) Ltd,
3 William Pickering Drive, Albany, Auckland.

Origination by Masterlith Ltd, Mitcham, Surrey

Printed and bound in Great Britain by Butler & Tanner Ltd,
Frome and London.

NANNY O.: I don't like abroad. I don't like the food and you can't trust the water and the Shamans always hog the deckchairs.

GRANNY W.: No, Gytha. Is Tuesday all right for you to meet?

NANNY O.: Well I'm baby-sitting on Tuesday; for our Jason's youngest. I can manage Friday. Hurry up with the tea, luv. I'm parched.

THE HORSE AND COACH CAREER THROUGH THE FOREST, CHASED BY THREE HORSEMEN.

COACH DRIVER: Come on!

9. CLEARING ON THE MOUNTAINSIDE. NIGHT.

MAGRAT IS POURING TEA.

GRANNY W.: You said your bit quite well. Just a bit more work on the screeching. Ain't that right, Nanny Ogg?

NANNY O.: Very useful screeching, I thought. And it's a good squint you've got there, too.

MAGRAT: Thank you. I've been practising.

GRANNY W.: A squint's only good if you can get your own eyes to stare up your nostrils.

MAGRAT: Would anyone care for a scone?

NANNY OGG AND GRANNY WEATHERWAX BOTH TAKE ONE.

GRANNY W.: They've got bats on.

MAGRAT: Yes! I made their eyes out of currants!

IN THE GREAT HALL IN LANCRE CASTLE THE GHOST RISES FROM VERENCE'S BODY. THE GHOST SURVEYS THE BODY AT HIS FEET.

VERENCE: Now, how did that...?

DEATH APPEARS.

DEATH: Hallo.

VERENCE: Hallo? *Hallo?!?* I am king, you know!

DEATH: *Was*, Your Majesty.

VERENCE: That's better. *(PAUSE)* What?

DEATH: I said was. It's called the past tense. You'll soon get used to it.

VERENCE: Who are you, fellow?

DEATH: Oh, I have many names.

VERENCE: Well, which one are you using at present?

DEATH: *Death* is as good as any.

VERENCE: Death. I see. So I'm...

DEATH: Yes.

> DEATH POINTS TO FELMET AND THE SHADOW OF LADY FELMET.

VERENCE: Oh. So it was Felmet. My father said I should never let him get behind me.

DEATH: *(SIGHS)* I suppose no-one mentioned anything to you?

VERENCE: Say again?

DEATH: No premonitions? Strange dreams? Mad old soothsayers shouting things at you in the street?

VERENCE: About what? Dying?

DEATH: *(SOURLY)* No. I suppose not. It would be too much to expect. They leave it all to me.

VERENCE: Who do?

DEATH: Fate. Destiny. All the rest of them.

> SEVERAL FOOTMEN ARRIVE AND CARRY THE CORPSE FROM THE HALL.

DEATH: The fact is, you're due to become a ghost.

VERENCE: *(FLATLY)* Oh.

DEATH: Don't let it upset you.

VERENCE: I'll try not to.

DEATH: Good man.

VERENCE: I don't think I'll be up to all that business with the white sheets and the chains, though.

10. THE FOREST. NIGHT.

> THE COACH RUSHES ALONG A TRACK PURSUED BY THE THREE RIDERS. ONE OF THEM FIRES A BOLT FROM A CROSSBOW.

COACH DRIVER: Come on!

11. LANCRE CASTLE. NIGHT.

VERENCE: Do I have to walk around moaning and screaming?

DEATH: Do you really want to?

VERENCE: No.

DEATH: Then I shouldn't bother, if I were you. And now, I really must be going.

DEATH STRIDES OFF THROUGH THE NEAREST WALL. VERENCE RUNS AFTER HIM, ALSO THROUGH THE WALL.

VERENCE: I say! Just hold on there! Is that all?

12. LANCRE CASTLE. NIGHT.

BINKY, DEATH'S HORSE, STANDS TETHERED TO THE BATTLEMENTS. DEATH EMERGES FROM THE CASTLE THROUGH A WALL, FOLLOWED BY VERENCE.

VERENCE: You can't just leave me like this! I...

VERENCE LOOKS BACK IN AMAZEMENT AT THE WALL.

VERENCE: Did... did I just walk through that?

13. THE FOREST. NIGHT.

THE CHASE BETWEEN THE COACH AND THE THREE HORSEMEN CONTINUES.

14. CLEARING IN THE FOREST. NIGHT.

GRANNY W.: Something comes.

MAGRAT: Can you tell by the pricking of your thumbs?

GRANNY W.: No, by the pricking of my ears.

THE COACH CAN BE HEARD DRAWING CLOSER.

NANNY O.: Hoofbeats? No-one would come up here this time of night.

MAGRAT: What's to be afraid of?

GRANNY W.: Us.

THE COACH CRASHES INTO THE CLEARING AND THE DRIVER LEAPS DOWN. HE OPENS THE DOOR, RETRIEVES A BUNDLE FROM THE INSIDE AND RUNS WITH IT TOWARDS THE WITCHES' FIRE. HE STOPS WHEN HE SEES GRANNY WEATHERWAX STANDING IN FRONT OF HIM.

GRANNY W.: It's all right.

A CROSSBOW BOLT THUDS INTO THE DRIVER'S BACK.

COACH DRIVER: Ugh!

HE MANAGES TO PASS THE BUNDLE TO GRANNY W. BEFORE HE FALLS PROSTRATE AT HER FEET. THREE SOLDIERS ARRIVE ON HORSEBACK AND DISMOUNT. THEY MARCH TOWARDS THE FIRE AND THE WITCHES. THE LEADER, BENTZEN, TAKES A COUPLE OF PACES IN FRONT OF THE OTHER TWO AND HOLDS OUT HIS HANDS FOR THE BUNDLE.

BENTZEN: Give that to me.

GRANNY W.: No.

BENTZEN: You are witches?

GRANNY W.: Ten out of ten for observation.

BENTZEN DRAWS HIS SWORD AND HOLDS IT OUT TOWARDS GRANNY W. SHE DOESN'T FLINCH. A FORK OF LIGHTNING JAGS DOWN FROM THE SKY AND HITS A CLUMP OF BUSHES, WHICH INCINERATE.

BENTZEN: Does the skin of witches turn aside steel?

GRANNY W.: Not that I'm aware. You could give it a try.

SOLDIER: With respect sir, it's not a good idea...

BENTZEN: Be silent. Your peasant magic is for fools, mother of the night. I can strike you down where you stand.

GRANNY W.: Then strike, man. If your heart tells you, strike as hard as you dare—

BENTZEN RAISES HIS SWORD AND AS HE DOES SO, ANOTHER FORK OF LIGHTNING JAGS DOWN AND HITS A ROCK A FEW YARDS AWAY.

BENTZEN: Missed.

HIS EYES CLOUD OVER AND HE FALLS AT GRANNY W.'S FEET. AS HE FALLS, HE REVEALS THE SOLDIER WHO STANDS BEHIND HIM, A DAGGER IN HIS HAND. GRANNY W. PRODS BENTZEN'S CORPSE WITH HER FOOT.

GRANNY W.: Perhaps you weren't aware of what I was aiming at. 'Mother of the night' indeed!

THE SOLDIER RUNS OFF.

THE 2ND SOLDIER HAS BEEN SLOWLY BACKING AWAY FROM THE SCENE.

SOLDIER: I didn't become a soldier for this! Not to go round killing people!

GRANNY W.: Exactly right. If I was you, I'd become a sailor. And now will someone tell me what all this is about?

MAGRAT: Perhaps they were bandits?

NANNY O.: No. They all wear the same badge. Anyone know what that means?

MAGRAT: It's the badge of King Verence!

GRANNY W.: Which king's he then?

MAGRAT: He rules this country.

GRANNY W.: Oh. That king.

NANNY OGG POINTS TO THE BUNDLE.

NANNY O.: What's that then?

THE BUNDLE GIVES A LITTLE CRY – THAT OF A BABY.

GRANNY W. UNWRAPS SOME OF THE CLOTH TO REVEAL THE CONTENTS. SHE LOOKS AT IT WITH SOME DISTASTE.

GRANNY W.: It's a baby.

SHE PASSES IT TO NANNY OGG.

NANNY O.: Oooh – goochy goo—

15. LANCRE CASTLE. DAWN.

DEATH AND VERENCE ARE STILL ON THE RAMPARTS.

VERENCE: Wait! You can't leave me like this!

DEATH: I can. You're undead, you see. It's not my responsibility.

VERENCE: But...

DEATH: Don't worry. It won't be forever.

VERENCE: Good.

DEATH: It will just *seem* like forever.

VERENCE: Won't anyone be able to see me?

DEATH: Oh, the psychically inclined. And cats of course...

VERENCE: I hate cats.

DEATH: Look, some people like to be ghosts. They can see how their descendants are getting on.

VERENCE: My son!

DEATH: Is something the matter?

VERENCE RUNS BACK INTO THE CASTLE THROUGH THE WALL.

DEATH: Don't mind me, will you.

DEATH MOUNTS BINKY.

DEATH: *(SIGHS)*

HE KICKS BINKY WITH HIS HEELS...

DEATH: Gee up, Binky!

...AND FLIES UP HIGH OVER THE FOREST. IN THE CLEARING BEYOND THE FOREST NANNY O. STILL HOLDS THE BABY AND IS LOOKING AT IT FONDLY.

SHE ROCKS THE BABY.

NANNY O.: Goochy goo!

GRANNY W.: *(WITH DERISION)* Goochy...?

SOMETHING FALLS OUT OF THE BUNDLE AND THUMPS TO THE GROUND AT MAGRAT'S FEET. SHE PICKS IT UP.

MAGRAT: It's a crown. It's got all spiky bits on it.

GRANNY W. TAKES THE CROWN FROM MAGRAT AND LOOKS AT IT ANXIOUSLY.

GRANNY W.: Oh dear.

MAGRAT: Hmmn?

GRANNY W.: I don't hold with looking at the future, but now I think the future's looking at me. And I don't like its expression at all!

16. LANCRE CASTLE. DAWN.

VERENCE: *(O.O.S.)* No!

VERENCE HAS RETURNED THROUGH THE WALL INTO THE CASTLE. HE IS STARING AT A STOUT WOODEN DOOR, BROKEN AND SPLINTERED.

VERENCE: Nooo!

HE RUNS INTO THE ROOM.

17. THE NURSERY. DAWN.

VERENCE RUNS ACROSS TO THE CRIB. IT IS EMPTY.

VERENCE: My son! Where is he?

HE BEGINS TO SEARCH FOR THE MISSING CHILD, THEN SEES A ROPE OF KNOTTED SHEETS DANGLING OUT OF THE WINDOW. HE RUNS OVER TO IT.

VERENCE: Revenge! I must find my son!

THE KNOTTED SHEET-ROPE DANGLES DOWN INTO THE COURTYARD BELOW. A HORSE STANDS TETHERED TO A POST IN THE COURTYARD.

18. LANCRE CASTLE. COURTYARD. DAWN.

VERENCE FLINGS HIMSELF THROUGH THE WINDOW, JUMPS DOWN ASTRIDE THE HORSE AND SINKS THROUGH IT. VERENCE DISENTANGLES HIMSELF.

VERENCE: Aaaaagh! I want revenge! I want my son.

HE RUNS TOWARDS THE GATES, BUT SLOWS TO A HALT, PANTING.

VERENCE: No! Trapped! Trapped!

ANOTHER GHOST, THAT OF KING CHAMPOT, APPROACHES.

CHAMPOT: Rotten night!

VERENCE: They don't come much rottener.

CHAMPOT: I couldn't help but notice... You can't leave, you see. You have to stay where you were killed. That's what haunting means. Take it from me. I know.

VERENCE: You can see me?

CHAMPOT: Oh yes. Quite clearly in fact.

VERENCE: Ah. You're a ghost too.

CHAMPOT: Well spotted.

VERENCE: It was the head under your arm. That gave me a clue.

CHAMPOT: Does it bother you? I can put it back on if it bothers you.

CHAMPOT EXTENDS HIS HAND.

CHAMPOT: Pleased to meet you. I'm Champot. King of Lancre.

VERENCE: Verence. Likewise. Don't seem to recall seeing your picture in the Long Gallery...

CHAMPOT: Oh, all that was after my time.

VERENCE: How long have you been here then?

CHAMPOT: Ooh about a thousand years... man and ghost.

VERENCE: *(AGHAST)* A thousand years!?!

CHAMPOT: Yes, I built this place, in fact. Just got it nicely decorated when my nephew cut my head off. There see...

THEY BEGIN TO WALK BACK TOWARDS THE CASTLE.

CHAMPOT: Can't tell you how much that upset me.

VERENCE: A thousand years?!

CHAMPOT: Still, it's not that bad. Better than being alive in many ways.

VERENCE: They must be very strange ways then! I *liked* being alive!

CHAMPOT: You'll be all right. You've got a strong morphogenic field.

VERENCE: What? What's that?

CHAMPOT: Hmmn... I was never very good with words – always found it easier to hit people with something...

VERENCE ENTERS THE CASTLE.

CHAMPOT: ...but I gather it all boils down to how alive you were. Something called animal vitality. The more you had the more you stay yourself, as it were. I expect you were one hundred percent alive, when you were alive.

INSIDE THE CASTLE, THEY LOOK DOWN INTO THE GREAT HALL.

VERENCE: Ah! Breakfast! Erm... how do we go about getting breakfast?

CHAMPOT: We don't. We're ghosts.

VERENCE: But I'm hungry!

CHAMPOT: You're not, you know. It's just your imagination.

19. THE GREAT HALL. MORNING.

DUKE FELMET AND HIS WIFE, LADY FELMET, ARE SITTING AT THE BREAKFAST TABLE.

LADY FELMET: I told Bentzen to have a word with the royal physician, and he agreed that Verence died of natural causes.

DUKE FELMET: Indeed, my love.

THE DUKE LOOKS OUT OF THE WINDOW.

LADY FELMET: *(V.O.)* I told him to say that falling down a flight of stairs with a dagger in your back was an incurable disease. A disease caused by unwise opening of the mouth. Rather good, I thought.

DUKE FELMET: Yes, my dear.

LADY FELMET: Though how you could have been so stupid as to let that fellow get away with the boy... That servant was far too loyal! I *told* you!

DUKE FELMET: Certainly, my dear.

LADY FELMET: I hope you... *What?!?*

DUKE FELMET: I'll have some cut down and brought in directly, my cherished.

LADY FELMET: Have some what cut down?

DUKE FELMET: Oh, the trees.

LADY FELMET: What have trees got to do with it?

DUKE FELMET: Well, there are such a lot of them.

LADY FELMET: Don't change the subject.

DUKE FELMET: Sorry, my sweet.

> AS LADY FELMET LEAVES, SHE WALKS THROUGH THE GHOST OF VERENCE WHO HAS RECENTLY ARRIVED WITH CHAMPOT.

LADY FELMET: You are impossible! And then there's the business of the crown! Where is it? And stop rubbing your hands!

> VERENCE GOES TO THE TABLE AND TRIES TO HELP HIMSELF TO THE COMESTIBLES.

VERENCE: Sausages. Bacon. Eggs. Smoked fish. Black pudding.

> CHAMPOT PLACES HIS HEAD ON THE TABLE.

CHAMPOT: You just *think* you're hungry.

VERENCE: I *think* I'm ravenous!

DUKE FELMET: Ha! Monarch of all I survey. And all I survey is trees. No blessed state of matrimony for them. Selfish bastards!

> THE COOK ENTERS.

COOK: Ahem. Is everything to your liking, majesty?

DUKE FELMET: Who are you?

COOK: The castle cook, majesty. Erm... is everything to...

DUKE FELMET: No. It isn't. Far too much meat for my liking. Take this away and bring me oatmeal. And a runny boiled egg.

VERENCE: Runny boiled egg?!?

> THE COOK PILES SEVERAL PLATES ON A TRAY HE HOLDS AND LEAVES THE ROOM. ON THE TOPMOST PLATTER SITS CHAMPOT'S HEAD. HIS BODY REMAINS SITTING AT THE TABLE.

VERENCE: I want some breakfast!!

20. LANCRE CASTLE. KITCHEN. MORNING.

> THE FOOL AND THE PORTER ARE PLAYING CARDS BY THE FIRE.

PORTER: Is Mr Bun the Baker at home?

> THE COOK ARRIVES WITH THE TRAY. HE DEPOSITS THE PLATES TOGETHER WITH CHAMPOT'S HEAD IN THE SINK.

CHAMPOT: A little more respect might be in order...

COOK: Oatmeal! And a runny boiled egg! S'not proper food is that! If you can't roast it and it doesn't have an apple in its mouth, I don't want to serve it.

> A THUNDEROUS KNOCKING AT THE GATEHOUSE DOOR.

PORTER: There is a knocking without.

FOOL: Without what?

PORTER: Without the door, idiot!

FOOL: A knocking without a door? This isn't some kind of Zen, is it?

PORTER: All right. All right. I'm coming!

COOK: What's a Zen?

FOOL: Oh, a sub-sect of the Turnwise Klatch philosophical system of Sumtin, an interesting aspect is the asking of apparently nonsensical questions in order to widen the doors of percep...

COOK: How's that again?

FOOL: Er... I'faith nuncle, thou't more full of questions than a martleberry is full of mizzensails.

COOK: Well, okay... And another thing. I kept getting the feeling that someone was trying to take the tray out of me hands. Funny that.

21. LANCRE CASTLE. GATEHOUSE. MORNING.

THE PORTER HAS ARRIVED AT THE DOOR WHICH IS SHAKING BENEATH THE TREMENDOUS KNOCKING. HE OPENS A LITTLE HATCH IN THE DOOR AND PEERS OUT.

THE 2ND SOLDIER STARES AT THE PORTER THROUGH THE HATCH.

PORTER: Who dost knock without?

2ND SOLDIER: Without? Without what?

PORTER: If you're going to muck about, you can stay without all day.

2ND SOLDIER: No! I must see the Duke this instant! Witches are abroad!

22. MAGRAT'S COTTAGE. DAY.

THE THREE WITCHES ARE SITTING TOGETHER.

NANNY OGG IS DANDLING THE BABY IN HER ARMS.

GRANNY WEATHERWAX LOOKS GRUMPILY AT THE BABY AND THEN AT THE CROWN WHICH SHE HOLDS IN HER HANDS.

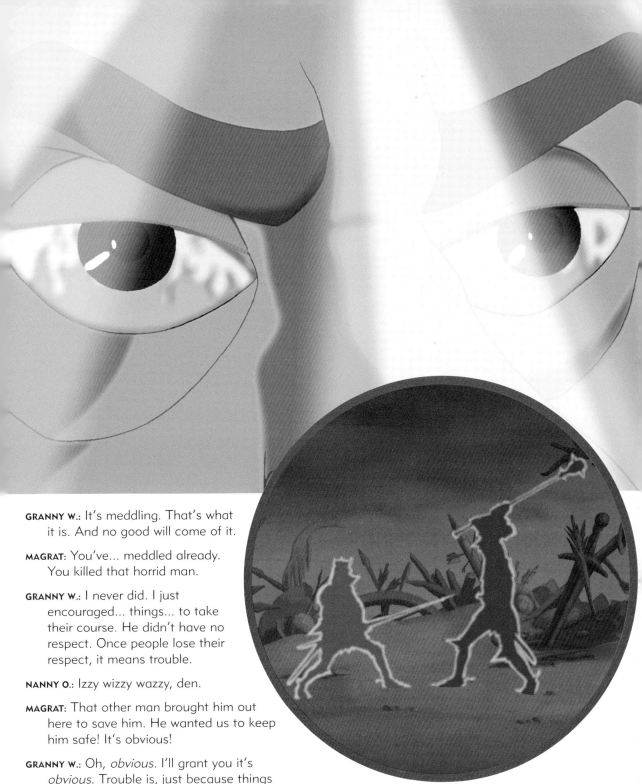

GRANNY W.: It's meddling. That's what it is. And no good will come of it.

MAGRAT: You've... meddled already. You killed that horrid man.

GRANNY W.: I never did. I just encouraged... things... to take their course. He didn't have no respect. Once people lose their respect, it means trouble.

NANNY O.: Izzy wizzy wazzy, den.

MAGRAT: That other man brought him out here to save him. He wanted us to keep him safe! It's obvious!

GRANNY W.: Oh, *obvious*. I'll grant you it's *obvious*. Trouble is, just because things are obvious, doesn't mean they're true.

MAGRAT: Yes, but the point is...

GRANNY W.: The point is that people are going to come looking. Serious people. Serious looking. Pull-down-the-walls and burn-off-the-thatch looking. And...

NANNY O.: Howsa boy, den?

GRANNY W.: *(IMPATIENTLY)* ...*And*, Gytha, I'm sure we'll all be a lot happier if you'd stop gurgling like that!

NANNY O.: You're not telling me how to look after a child. And me with fifteen of my own?

GRANNY W.: I'm just saying that we ought to think about it.

MAGRAT: Well?

GRANNY W.: First we've got to take him away from here. A long way away where no-one knows who he is.

SHE LOOKS AT THE CROWN.

GRANNY W.: And then there's this.

MAGRAT: Oh, that's easy. I mean, you just hide it under a stone or something. Much easier than babies.

GRANNY W.: It ain't. The reason being the country's full of babies and they all look the same. But I don't reckon there's many crowns. They have this way of being found. They kind of call out to people's minds. If you bunged it under a stone up here, in a week's time it'd get itself discovered by accident. You mark my words.

NANNY O.: It's true, that is. How many times have you flung a magic ring into the deepest depths of the ocean and then, when you get home and have a nice bit of turbot for your tea, there it is?

GRANNY W.: Never. And nor have you. Anyway, he might want it back. Kings set a lot of store by crowns. Really Gytha. Sometimes you say the most...

MAGRAT: (*BRIGHTLY*) I'll just make some tea, shall I?

SHE GOES OUT.

NANNY O.: She done it up nice, hasn't she. Flowers and everything. What are them things on the walls?

GRANNY W.: Sigils... Or some such.

NANNY O.: Fancy.

GRANNY W.: Modern. When I was a gel, we had a lump of wax and a couple of pins and we had to be content. We had to make our *own* enchantment in them days.

NANNY O.: Ah. Well, we've all passed a lot of water since then.

GRANNY WEATHERWAX SNIFFS.

GRANNY W.: What's that smell?

NANNY O. LIFTS THE BABY AND STUDIES A DAMP PATCH ON HER SKIRT.

NANNY O.: Ah. I'll just go and see if Magrat has any clean rags, shall I?

SHE LEAVES THE ROOM. GRANNY W. IS LEFT ALONE WITH THE CROWN. SLOWLY SHE PUTS IT ON. SHE GESTURES IMPERIOUSLY.

GRANNY W.: Jolly well do this! Chop his head off, what ho!

THE WALLS BEHIND HER FADE AND ARE REPLACED BY A MONTAGE OF TERRIBLE BATTLES AND DARK DEEDS. WITH NO LITTLE EFFORT, GRANNY REMOVES THE CROWN FROM HER HEAD. THE BRUTAL SCENES FADE AND THE WALLS OF MAGRAT'S COTTAGE REAPPEAR ONCE AGAIN. GRANNY PLACES THE CROWN ON THE TABLE NEARBY.

GRANNY W.: So, that's being a king for you, is it? I wonder why they all want the job?

MAGRAT: *(AIRILY – A LITTLE SHRILL)* Sugar?

GRANNY W.: Three spoons... You'd have to be a born fool to be a king.

MAGRAT: Sorry?

MAGRAT IS LOOKING AT THE CROWN. GRANNY W. NOTICES HER FIXED STARE.

GRANNY W.: You can feel it, can you? I said, didn't I. Crowns call out.

MAGRAT: It's horrible. It's trying to get me to try it on.

GRANNY W.: It does that. Yes.

MAGRAT: But I shall be strong. Like you.

GRANNY W.: So I should think – sniff—

MAGRAT: It's not as though it looks much like a crown. Just a thin little thing.

GRANNY W.: You've seen a lot of them I expect. You'd be an expert on them, naturally.

MAGRAT: Seen a fair few. They've got a lot more jewels on them. And cloth bits in the middle. When I was being trained up by Goodie Whemper...

GRANNY W.: Maysherestinpeace.

MAGRAT: ...maysherestinpeace, she used to take me into Lancre whenever the strolling players were in town. She was very keen on the theatre. And they've got more crowns than you can shake a stick at. Although, mind, Goodie did say they're made of tin and paper and stuff. But they look more realler than this one. Do you think that's strange?

GRANNY W.: Things that try to look like things often do look more like things than things. Well-known fact. But I don't hold with encouraging it. What do they stroll about playing then, in these crowns?

MAGRAT: Don't you know about the theatre?

GRANNY W.: Oh yes. It's one of *them* style of things, then, is it? Good people are they, these theatre players?

MAGRAT: I think so.

GRANNY W.: And they stroll around the country, you say?

MAGRAT: All over the place. There's a troupe of them in Lancre now, I hear.

GRANNY W.: Right. Go and tell Gytha to wrap the baby up well. It's a long time since I heard a theatre played properly.

23. THE CASTLE THRONE ROOM. DAY.

THE DUKE AND LADY FELMET ARE SITTING ON THEIR THRONES.

> **DUKE FELMET:** *(V.O.)* Witches?
>
> **LADY FELMET:** *(V.O.)* Witches?!?

THEY ARE HOLDING AUDIENCE WITH THE CHAMBERLAIN. A COUPLE OF SOLDIERS LOOK ON, AS DOES VERENCE.

VERENCE: Witches?

IN THE BACKGROUND CHAMPOT SEARCHES FOR HIS MISSING HEAD.

LADY FELMET: Where I come from, we don't allow witches. And we don't propose to allow them here. You will furnish us with their addresses.

CHAMBERLAIN: Addresses, ladyship?

DUKE FELMET: Where they live. I trust your tax gatherers know where to find them?

CHAMPOT WALKS THROUGH THE CHAMBERLAIN ON HIS WAY OUT.

CHAMBERLAIN: Ah.

DUKE FELMET: I trust that they do pay taxes.

CHAMBERLAIN: Not exactly *pay* taxes, my lord.

DUKE FELMET: Go on, man.

CHAMBERLAIN: Well, it's more that they don't pay, you see. We never felt, that is, the old king didn't think... well, they just don't.

DUKE FELMET: I see. Very well. You may go.

> THE CHAMBERLAIN GOES OUT.

LADY FELMET: That was how your family used to run a kingdom, was it? *(BRUSQUELY)* You had a positive duty to kill your cousin. It was clearly in the interests of the species. The weak don't deserve to survive!

> VERENCE SWIPES AT LADY FELMET. HIS FIST PASSES RIGHT THROUGH HER.

DUKE FELMET: Quite so, my passion.

24. LANCRE. MARKET PLACE. DAY.

> THE STROLLING PLAYERS ARE PERFORMING A PLAY ABOUT KING CHAMPOT. ONE ACTOR STABS ANOTHER. THE VICTORIOUS ACTOR – VITOLLER (PLAYING THE PART OF KING CHAMPOT) – LOOKS AT HIS DEFEATED FOE.

VITOLLER: So die all foes of Lancre!

ACTOR: Aaagh!

> GRANNY WEATHERWAX, NANNY OGG AND MAGRAT GARLICK ARE IN THE AUDIENCE.

GRANNY W.: He's killed him! And right up there in front of everyone!

MAGRAT: It's all right! He's not really dead!

GRANNY W.: Are you calling me a liar, my girl? I saw it all!

MAGRAT: Look, Granny. It's not really real, d'you see?

VITOLLER: Oh woe, woe, woe! Thrice woe!
For it is my brother I have kill'd!
Full twenty years and more have I
This country search'd for sight of thee
And now cruel fate has dealt a telling blow!

By mine own hand my brother's slain;
The worms will take his body as
Damned thoughts will claim my brain!

GRANNY W.: What's he on about now?

MAGRAT: He's saying how sorry he is the other man's dead. There's a lot of crowns, isn't there.

GRANNY W.: What'd he go and kill him for then?

MAGRAT: Well, it's a bit complicated...

NANNY O.: I reckon it's all pretending. Look. He's still breathing.

GRANNY W.: And look at his boots, too. A real king'd be ashamed of boots like those.

VITOLLER AND THE 'DEAD' ACTOR ARE JOINED ONSTAGE BY VARIOUS THESPIAN DUKES, EARLS, ETC.

THE PLAY HAS GROUND TO A HALT AND ALL THE ACTORS, INCLUDING THE CORPSE, ARE NOW STARING OPEN-MOUTHED AT THE WITCHES.

GRANNY W.: I don't know what you're staring at. Get on with it.

NANNY O. PROFFERS A BROWN PAPER BAG TO GRANNY W

NANNY O.: Have a humbug.

THE DUKE OF RAZORBACK HAS THE NEXT LINE, BUT HAS FORGOTTEN IT. HWEL EMERGES FROM THE WINGS AND HISSES A PROMPT.

HWEL: Oh who hath slain the prince, my Lord...

DUKE OF R.: Oh who... who... who hath slain... erm...

HWEL: ...the prince, my Lord!

DUKE OF R.: ...my Lord... er...

GRANNY W.: There's a man over on the side there whispering to them.

> **MAGRAT:** He's a prompter. He tells them what to say.
>
> **GRANNY W.:** Don't they know?
>
> **MAGRAT:** I think they're forgetting. For some reason!
>
> **DUKE OF R.:** And from whence hath come this benighted soul.
>
> He your brother was! His helmet hid his face!

YOUTH: Ah me! What foul and nasty deed
Here lies before us and by whom
Was this brave prince so untimely slain
That sleeps the long and dreamless sleep of death?

VITOLLER: Aye! And yet his death smites me full sore.

Hear me, my friends! For this I swear;

No more the King of Lancre I.

By mine own sword I now shall die!

DUKE OF R.: No, no! This shall not be!

Knowst thou not what heresy

Thou commit'st here?

VITOLLER: Thou speakest true. To act as judge and jury

On mine own immortal soul is not my charge;

'Tis for he above and he alone

And by his grace I shall atone.

GRANNY W.: What's this bit?

MAGRAT: *(SIGHS)* That's the king's daughter...

GRANNY W.: It never is. It's a man. In a straw wig. Making his voice squeaky.

MAGRAT: Yes. But it's the theatre, see. All the women are played by men.

GRANNY W.: Why?

MAGRAT: They don't allow no women on the stage.

> A MAN IN THE ROW BEHIND GRANNY TAPS HER ON THE SHOULDER.

MAN: Madam, will you kindly remove your hat?

GRANNY W.: No. What's going on now?

NANNY O.: They're talking about him who's dead. I think they're wondering who killed him.

GRANNY W.: Are they! Indeed!

> SHE STANDS UP AND POINTS AN ACCUSATORY FINGER AT THE CAST.

GRANNY W.: He done it! We all seed him! He done it with a dagger!

25. LANCRE CASTLE. DAY.

> THE DUKE AND LADY FELMET ARE IN THE MAIN HALL.

DUKE FELMET: Of course, there would appear to be many witches. It might be difficult to find the three that were on the moor.

LADY FELMET: That doesn't matter.

DUKE FELMET: Of course not.

LADY FELMET: Put matters in hand.

DUKE FELMET: Yes, my passion.

> AT THE TABLE VERENCE HAS MANAGED TO LIFT A GRAIN OF SALT.

VERENCE: Ha! Now we shall see!

> CHAMPOT'S HEAD SPEAKS TO HIM FROM A FRUIT STAND ON THE TABLE.

CHAMPOT: I don't suppose you've seen my body about have you?

> THE GRAIN OF SALT FALLS THROUGH VERENCE'S HAND.

VERENCE: You made me drop it!

26. LANCRE. MARKET PLACE. DAY.

GRANNY W., NANNY O. AND MAGRAT HAVE STAYED BEHIND WHILE THE REST OF THE AUDIENCE HAVE LEFT. THEY ARE STILL IN THEIR SEATS.

GRANNY W.: I wonder how they manage to get all them kings and lords to come here and do this? I'd have thought they'd been too busy. Ruling and similar.

MAGRAT: No, I still don't think you quite understand.

GRANNY W.: Well, I'm going to get to the bottom of it.

SHE GOES TO THE STAGE AND PULLS BACK THE CURTAIN. SHE FINDS HERSELF STARING AT WHAT HAD LATELY BEEN THE CORPSE OF KING CHAMPOT'S BROTHER.

GRANNY W.: You! You're dead!

HE FALLS BACK OFF HIS CHAIR IN A DEAD FAINT.

GRANNY W. FINDS HERSELF CONFRONTED BY VITOLLER.

VITOLLER: May I assist you, good ladies?

GRANNY W.: I know you. You done the murder. Leastways, it looked like it.

VITOLLER: So glad. It is always a pleasure to meet a true connoisseur. Olwyn Vitoller at your service. Manager of this band of vagabonds.

GRANNY W.: Yes. Well.

NANNY O.: I thought you was very good too. The way you shouted all them words so graciously. I could tell you was a king.

MAGRAT: I hope we didn't upset things.

VITOLLER: My dear lady. Could I begin to tell you how gratifying it is for a mere mummer to learn that his audience has seen beneath the shell of greasepaint to the spirit below?

GRANNY W.: I expect you could say anything, Mr Vitoller.

VITOLLER: And now, to what do I owe this visit from three such charming ladies?

GRANNY W.: We'd like to talk to you, Mr Vitoller. Somewhere private.

VITOLLER: Dear lady, but of a certain. Currently I have lodgings in yonder esteemed watering hole.

MAGRAT: You mean... in the pub?

27. LANCRE MARKET PLACE. THE PUB. DAY.

THE SOUND OF ROISTERING CAN BE HEARD COMING FROM THE PUB. IT IS FULL AND VERY NOISY. IN ONE CORNER SIT NANNY O. AND GRANNY W.

AT THE OTHER END OF THEIR TABLE, MR AND MRS VITOLLER ARE COUNTING THE AFTERNOON'S TAKINGS.

GRANNY W.: I don't want this to end up with your usual dancing on the table, showing your petticoats and singing about how 'The Hedgehog can never be Whatsnamed At All'.

GRANNY W. LOOKS TOWARDS VITOLLER AND HWEL.

GRANNY W.: You see there is this child. And he needs a home...

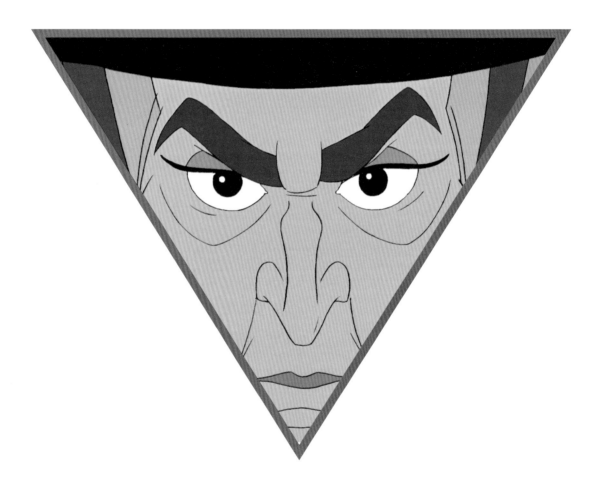

1. LANCRE CASTLE. DAY.

DUKE FELMET: *(V.O.)* Bring me a witch.

2. LANCRE CASTLE. GREAT HALL. DAY.

DUKE FELMET, THE FOOL, A SERGEANT, THREE SOLDIERS AND THE GHOST OF VERENCE ARE PRESENT.

CHAMPOT IS SEARCHING FOR THE HEAD HE LOST EARLIER. THIS IS SITTING IN A LARGE HELPING OF TREACLE SPONGE AND CUSTARD.

DUKE FELMET: In chains if necessary.

SERGEANT: Sir!

CHAMPOT'S HEAD SPOTS HIS BODY AND CALLS TO IT.

CHAMPOT: I say! Here body! Over here! Good body! Fetch! Over here!

DUKE FELMET: Well, go on man! Look lively!

SERGEANT: Sir!

HE BECKONS A GROUP OF SOLDIERS TO FOLLOW HIM. CHAMPOT'S BODY FINDS THE HEAD AND PICKS IT UP.

CHAMPOT: Steady! Mind my eye!

THE DUKE SITS AT TABLE AND TAKES A SPOONFUL OF SOUP, WHICH HE INSTANTLY SPITS OUT.

DUKE FELMET: Ptaaaghh!

3. LANCRE TOWN SQUARE. DAY.

INSIDE THE PUB, GRANNY W. IS DISCUSSING THE MATTER OF THE FOUNDLING (IN NANNY OGG'S ARMS) WITH VITOLLER AND MRS VITOLLER.

GRANNY W.: You see there is this child. And he needs a home...

HWEL: Why does he need a home?

GRANNY W.: He hasn't got one. At least, not one where he would be welcome.

VITOLLER: This is no life for a child; always moving. Always a new town. And no room for schooling. They say that's very important these days.

HWEL: And you are by way of being his...

NANNY O.: Godmothers.

4. LANCRE MARKET SQUARE. DAY.

THE STAGE IS DESERTED. MAGRAT HOLDS A BAG CONTAINING THE CROWN WHICH, TOGETHER WITH THE BABY, HAD BEEN DELIVERED TO THE WITCHES EARLIER. SHE IS LOOKING AROUND FOR SOMEWHERE TO HIDE IT. IN A PROPS BOX SHE FINDS HATS AND CROWNS. SHE TAKES SOME OF THE CONTENTS OUT, THEN REMOVES THE CROWN FROM HER BAG. SHE STUDIES IT BRIEFLY.

MAGRAT: Hoo! You look really tatty compared to the others.

SHE PUSHES THE CROWN DOWN AMONGST THE CONTENTS OF THE BOX.

MAGRAT: Hoogh.

ONE OF THE ACTORS APPROACHES HER FROM BEHIND AND GOOSES HER.

MAGRAT: Wooogh!!

ACTOR: Hallo, my lovely. What are you doing tonight?

MAGRAT: Nothing! I mean... I... oooh!

SHE RUNS OFF, COVERED IN CONFUSION.

5. PUBLIC HOUSE. DAY.

VITOLLER: We should be happy to take care of him.

GRANNY W. PUTS MONEY ON THE TABLE.

GRANNY W.: This should take care of... nappies and suchlike. Whatever.

VITOLLER: A hundred times over, I should think! Why didn't you mention this before?

GRANNY W.: If I had to buy you, you wouldn't be worth the price.

NANNY O. HANDS THE BUNDLE OVER TO MRS VITOLLER.

HWEL: There's something else here, isn't there. Something big behind all this.

GRANNY W. NODS.

HWEL: But... it would do us no good at all to know it?

GRANNY W. NODS AGAIN.

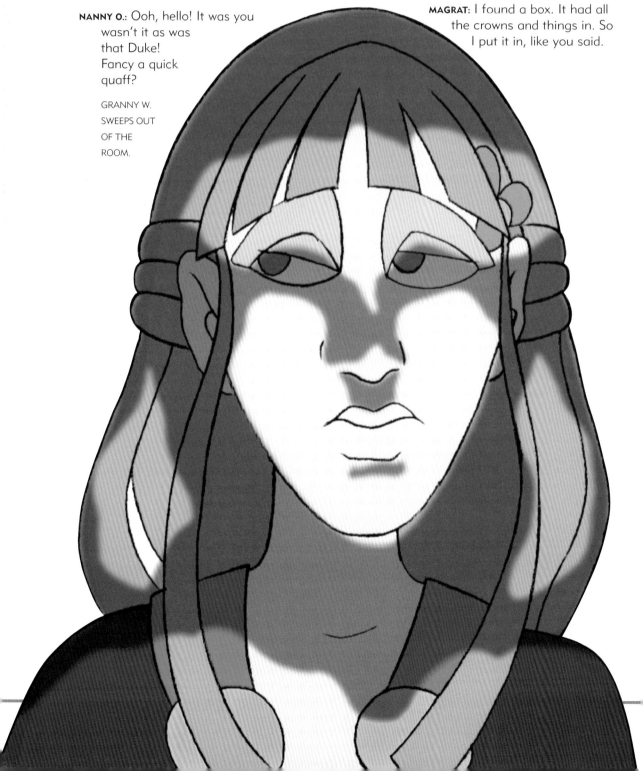

GRANNY W.: I have other things to see to. Please excuse me.

VITOLLER: What's his name?

THE TWO WITCHES REPLY IN UNISON.

GRANNY W.: Tom.
NANNY O.: John. *(TOGETHER)*

GRANNY W.: Tom John.

GRANNY W. AND NANNY O. WALK TOWARDS THE TAVERN DOOR. AS THEY REACH IT, A COUPLE OF THE ACTORS COME IN.

NANNY O.: Ooh, hello! It was you wasn't it as was that Duke! Fancy a quick quaff?

GRANNY W. SWEEPS OUT OF THE ROOM.

6. LANCRE MARKET SQUARE. DAY.

MAGRAT HAS REACHED THE PUB DOOR. GRANNY W. COMES OUT OF THE PUB.

GRANNY W.: Well?

MAGRAT: Where's Nanny Ogg?

GRANNY W.: She's quaffing. Ale.

MAGRAT: Quaffing?

GRANNY W.: It's like drinking only you spill more. What about the crown?

MAGRAT: I found a box. It had all the crowns and things in. So I put it in, like you said.

GRANNY W.: Did anyone see you?

MAGRAT: No. Everyone was too busy. But...

GRANNY W.: Out with it, girl.

MAGRAT: A man came up and pinched my bum!

GRANNY W.: Did he! And then what?

MAGRAT: And... and... I don't know! It never happened before.

GRANNY W.: Goodie Whemper...

MAGRAT: Maysherestinpeace.

GRANNY W.: Maysherestinpeace, yes. She didn't get out and about much, did she.

MAGRAT: It was her leg, you know.

GRANNY W.: But she taught you all the midwifery and everything.

MAGRAT: Oh yes; *that*. I done lots.

GRANNY W.: But... erm... she never talked about what you might call the... the *previous*.

MAGRAT: Sorry?

GRANNY W.: You know... Men... and such.

MAGRAT: What about them?

GRANNY W.: Well... Hoogh! I think it might be a good idea if you have a quiet word with Nanny Ogg one of these days. Fairly soon.

NANNY O.: *(O.O.S.)* Oh... the sheep is a jolly companion,

So long as you're wearing a boot.

And I've heard that you can with an orang utan,

So long as you ply it with fruit.

If your passion is rabbit, then reach out and grab it,

And lettuce works well as a rule.

If you fancy a laugh, then try a giraffe,

But remember, you'll need a tall stool.

There is only one single exception,

An animal, spiny and small...

Oh the hedgehog can never,

The hedgehog can never,

The hedgehog can never be bothered at all!

GRANNY W. LEADS MAGRAT AWAY FROM THE PUB.

GRANNY W.: Only not just now.

7. LANCRE CASTLE. EVENING.

> THE SERGEANT, TOGETHER WITH HIS THREE
> SOLDIERS, RIDES OUT OF THE CASTLE.
>
> THE GHOSTS OF CHAMPOT AND VERENCE THEN GO.

VERENCE: Oh, how I wish I could go hunting. Used to live for it, you know.

8. THE TOWN OF LANCRE. EVENING.

> THE TRAVELLING PLAYERS' CARTS LEAVE THE TOWN.

9. MAGRAT'S COTTAGE. NIGHT.

> MAGRAT AND GRANNY W. ARE LOOKING INTO
> NANNY OGG'S CRYSTAL BALL.

GRANNY W.: It's about time you learned how to get sound on this thing.

MAGRAT: Where's Nanny?

GRANNY W.: She's lying out on the lawn. She felt a bit... poorly.

NANNY O.: *(O.O.S.)* 'Oh the wizard has ancient and wrinkly hands,

His legs are knobbly and bowed,

His beard is long and an odorous pong

Follows him a-all around.

His clothing is tattered and dirty,

His nose is decidedly bent.

But the wizard's staff is four foot and a half.

And it's got a big knob on the end!' Hee hee hee hee!

MAGRAT: You know, if we *are* to be his god-mothers, we ought to give him three gifts. It's traditional.

GRANNY W.: What are you talking about, girl?

MAGRAT: Three good witches are supposed to give the baby three gifts. You know, like good looks, wisdom and happiness. That's how it used to be done in the old days.

GRANNY W.: Oh, you mean gingerbread cottages and all that. Spinning wheels and pumpkins and pricking your finger on a rose thorn and similar. I could never be having with all that.

MAGRAT: Yes, but...

GRANNY W.: Hoogh! Oh well, if it makes you any happier... What's it to be? Wealth? Beauty?

MAGRAT: Well, money isn't everything. And if he takes after his father he'll be handsome enough... erm... Perfect eyesight? A good singing voice?

NANNY O.: (O.O.S.) 'Oooooh the wizard's staff is four foot and a half,

And it's got a big knob on the end!'

GRANNY W.: Not important... You've got to think headology, you see. Not muck about with all this wealth and beauty business.

NANNY OGG ENTERS.

NANNY O.: Wotcha Esme! What are you two up to then, eh?

10. THE FOREST. NIGHT.

THE SERGEANT AND SOLDIERS DISPATCHED BY DUKE FELMET TO CAPTURE A WITCH ARE RIDING THROUGH THE TREES.

SOLDIER 1: How are you supposed to go about arresting a witch?

SOLDIER 2: I don't know. Don't think she'd like the idea, though.

SOLDIER 1: No. And I don't like the idea of her not liking the idea.

11. MAGRAT'S COTTAGE. NIGHT.

NANNY O.: Three gifts eh? Haven't done one of them things since I was a gel. Takes me back... What're you doing?

MAGRAT: Oh, we've got to create the right magical ambience.

NANNY O.: What are we going to give him then?

GRANNY W.: We was just discussing it.

NANNY O.: I know what he'll want! Hee hee hee!

SHE WHISPERS TO MAGRAT.

MAGRAT: I don't see what use *that* would be. Wouldn't it be rather uncomfortable?

GRANNY W.: Something a bit less physical is generally the style of things!

NANNY O.: He'll thank us for it when he grows up.

MAGRAT: I think that perhaps it would be a good idea if we all do it in our own way. You know. Separately. It's been a long day and we're all rather tired.

GRANNY W.: *(BRUSQUELY)* Good idea! Come, Nanny Ogg! It's been a long day and we're all rather... *tired*!

THEY MAKE THEIR WAY OUT OF THE COTTAGE.

NANNY O.: Speak for yourself. I'm ready for anything! Hee hee!

GRANNY W.: Ready for the mother and father of a headache tomorrow morning!

NANNY O.: Are you suggesting that I've drunk too much?

GRANNY W.: Yes.

MAGRAT SITS DOWN AT THE TABLE.

MAGRAT: Oh well. I suppose I could make a start. He will makes friends easily... something I've never been able to get the hang of...

12. NANNY O.'S COTTAGE. NIGHT.

NANNY O. SITS IN HER KITCHEN.

NANNY O.: Oh when I was a lass and a pretty one too,

I met a young soldier boy who... who... erm... oh.

How's it go?
...A good memory is what he ought to have. He'll always remember the words.

13. THE FOREST. NIGHT.

THE SERGEANT AND SOLDIERS APPROACH AND DISMOUNT.

SOLDIER 3: What now sarge?

SERGEANT: We... we spread out. Yes. We spread out. That's what we do.

SERGEANT CROUCHES BEHIND A LARGE LOG.

SERGEANT: Wha...?

HE TURNS TO FIND HIS THREE MEN ALL CROUCHING BEHIND HIM.

SERGEANT: Right. Very good. You've got the general idea. Now. Let's spread out again. And this time we spread out separately.

14. THE FOREST. NIGHT.

GRANNY W. APPEARS.

GRANNY W.: Let him be whoever he thinks he is. That's all anybody could hope for in this world.

SHE TRUDGES ON THROUGH THE TREES.

15. THE FOREST. NIGHT.

THE SERGEANT LOOKS NERVOUSLY AT THE COTTAGE.

SERGEANT: Right. Now we...

HE TRIES TO SPEAK MORE QUIETLY.

SERGEANT: We... erm... oh 'eck.

HE WALKS TO THE COTTAGE AND KNOCKS AT THE BACK DOOR.

SERGEANT: *(JAUNTILY)* No-one in. Blast.

THE DOOR SEEMS TO BE OPENING BY ITSELF.

SERGEANT: Ahem. Ahem.

GRANNY W. APPEARS AS IF FROM NOWHERE.

GRANNY W.: That's a nasty cough you've got there.

SERGEANT: Aaagh!

GRANNY W.: You did right in coming to me.

SERGEANT: Argle!

16. LANCRE CASTLE. MORNING.

DUKE FELMET: *(V.O.)* She did *what*?!?

17. LANCRE CASTLE. MORNING.

IN THE GREAT HALL, THE DUKE SITS AT BREAKFAST. THE SERGEANT STANDS TO ATTENTION. THE FOOL SITS ON A SMALL STOOL. THE GHOST OF KING VERENCE IS PUSHING A PEA DOWN THE TABLE.

SERGEANT: She gave me a cup of tea, sir.

DUKE FELMET: And what about your men?

SERGEANT: She gave them one too, sir.

DUKE FELMET: Sergeant?

SERGEANT: Sir?

DUKE FELMET: I'm not sure I made your orders clear, sergeant.

SERGEANT: Sir?

DUKE FELMET: I mean it is possible I may have confused you. I meant to say 'Bring me a witch, in chains if necessary', but perhaps what I really said was 'Go and have a cup of tea.' Was this in fact the case?

SERGEANT: Erm... No sir.

DUKE FELMET: I wonder why, then, you did not in fact do this thing I asked?

SERGEANT: Sir?

DUKE FELMET: I expect she said some magic words, did she? I imagine she offered you visions of unearthly delight? Did she show you dark fascinations and forbidden raptures, the like of which mortal men should not even think of? And demonic secrets that took you to the depths of man's desires?

SERGEANT: Are you all right sir?

DUKE FELMET: What? Oh, perfectly, perfectly.

SERGEANT: Only you've gone all red.

DUKE FELMET: Don't change the subject, man! Admit it. She offered you hedonistic and licentious pleasures known only to those who dabble in the carnal arts, didn't she?

SERGEANT: *(FIRMLY)* No sir. She offered me a bun.

DUKE FELMET: A... a bun?

SERGEANT: Yes sir. It had currants in it.

DUKE FELMET: And what did your men do about this?

SERGEANT: They had a bun too sir. Well, all except Roger, who isn't allowed fruit, sir, on account of his trouble. He had a biscuit, sir.

DUKE FELMET: You may go, sergeant.

SERGEANT: Sir!

HE MARCHES OUT.

18. NANNY O.'S COTTAGE. NIGHT.

GRANNY W. FLIES DOWN TOWARDS THE GARDEN IN FRONT OF THE COTTAGE.

GRANNY W.: Steady... Steady, I said!

19. LANCRE CASTLE. NIGHT.

DUKE FELMET: Fool?

FOOL: Marry, sir...

LADY FELMET ENTERS.

DUKE FELMET: I am already extremely married. Advise me, my Fool.

FOOL: I'faith, nuncle.

DUKE FELMET: Nor am I thy nuncle. I feel sure I would have remembered. If you preface your next remark with nuncle, i'faith or marry, it will go hard with you.

FOOL: How do you feel about prithee?

LADY FELMET: You come from these parts, don't you.

FOOL: Marr... yes, ma'am.

LADY FELMET: So you would know all about the native beliefs and so on?

FOOL: I suppose so, ma'am.

DUKE FELMET: Where do you sleep, my Fool?

FOOL: In the stables, sir.

DUKE FELMET: From now on you may sleep in the corridor outside my room.

FOOL: Gosh! Thanks.

LADY FELMET: Now... Tell us all about the witches.

20. NANNY O.'S COTTAGE. NIGHT.

NANNY O. AND MAGRAT ARE SITTING TOGETHER.

GRANNY W.: *(O.O.S.)* Wooaah! Drat the dratted... Good evening.

MAGRAT: Well met by moonlight. Merry meet. A star shines on...

NANNY O.: Wotcha.

GRANNY W. SITS DOWN TOO. SHE NOTICES MAGRAT'S HAIR.

GRANNY W.: What you done to your hair, girl? Looks like a window box has fallen on your head.

MAGRAT: Yes. Well. Anyway. If we're going to start, we'd better light the candles.

NANNY O.: But we got this lovely new lamp our Tracie sent me. And I was going to poke up the fire a bit.

MAGRAT PRODUCES A LARGE PIECE OF CHALK.

NANNY O.: You ain't going to draw on the floor again, neither. Took our Dreen days to clean up all those wossnames last time.

MAGRAT: Runes. Look, just one candle?

NANNY O.: Oh, all right, if it makes you feel any better. Just the one, mind. And a decent white one. Nothing fancy. What about this new king, then?

MAGRAT: Had some people executed in Lancre the other day for saying as how he killed King Verence. Spreading malicious lies, he said. He said Verence died of natural causes.

GRANNY W.: Well, being assassinated *is* natural causes for a king. Had some houses burned down in Bad Ass, too. Because of taxes.

NANNY O.: Old King Verence used to do that. Terrible temper he had.

GRANNY W.: *He* used to let people out first, though.

NANNY O.: Oh yes. He could be very gracious like that.

GRANNY W.: And every Hogswatch night, a side of venison. Regular.

NANNY O.: Oh yes. Very respectful to witches he was... And then there was that great hairy thing of his.

GRANNY W.: Ah. His droit de seigneur.

NANNY O.: Needed a lot of exercise.

MAGRAT: What are you talking about? Did he keep pets?

GRANNY W.: I think we might have to keep an eye on this new one, though. I think he might be a bit clever. That's not a good thing in a king. And I don't think he knows how to show respect.

MAGRAT: A man came to see me last week and asked me if I wanted to pay any taxes. I told him no.

NANNY O.: Came to see me too. But our Jason and our Wayne went out and tole him we didn't want to join.

GRANNY W.: Small man? Bald, black cloak?

MAGRAT & NANNY O.: Yes.

GRANNY W.: He was hanging about in my raspberry bushes. Only when I went out to see what he wanted, he ran away.

MAGRAT: Actually, I gave him tuppence. He said he was going to be tortured, you see, if he didn't get witches to pay their taxes...

21. Lancre Castle. Night.

DUKE FELMET SITS ON HIS THRONE. LADY FELMET STANDS BESIDE HIM. VERENCE IS TRYING TO MOVE A SMALL, TWO-PRONGED FORK. THE TAXMAN STANDS NEARBY.

LADY FELMET: Well?

TAXMAN: Well, ma'am, you see. I explained about the need to employ a standing army, ekcetra, and I mentioned how taxes help to maintain the King's Peace, ekcetra... ma'am... ekcetra...

LADY FELMET: And?

TAXMAN: They said the king should maintain his own peace ma'am. And then they gave me a look.

DUKE FELMET: What sort of a look?

TAXMAN: It's sort of hard to describe.

DUKE FELMET: Try.

TAXMAN: Well... it... wasn't nice.

DUKE FELMET: Not nice.

TAXMAN: No sir. You're... you're not going to make me go back are you?

DUKE FELMET: No, no. Just call in on the torturer on your way out. See when he can fit you in.

TAXMAN: Yes sir. At once, sir. Thank you sir!

THE TAXMAN LEAVES THE ROOM.

22. Vitoller's Cart. Evening.

AT A TABLE, HWEL IS WRITING. VITOLLER IS TRYING TO DECIDE WHAT PLAY TO GIVE THE RESIDENTS OF QUIRM ON THE FOLLOWING AFTERNOON. TOMJON IS BENEATH THE TABLE PLAYING WITH A BOX OF PROPS.

VITOLLER: All right. How about 'The King's Brides'?

HWEL: Last year.

VITOLLER: Then we'll give them 'Mallo the Tyrant of Klatch'! 'In blood I came! And by blood rule.'

HWEL: We did that the year before. Anyway. People are fed up with kings. They want a bit of a chuckle.

VITOLLER: They are not fed up with my kings! My dear boy! People come to the theatre to Experience. To Learn. To Wonder!

HWEL STANDS UP AND PASSES THE MANUSCRIPT TO VITOLLER.

HWEL: To laugh. Here. Have a look at this one. See? Look there. The comic gravediggers. And I found room for the star-crossed lovers, too. And the hunchback king.

HWEL: It's the cats and the roller skates. They're the trouble.

VITOLLER LEAVES.

TOMJON: Ha Ha.

HE HAS DISCOVERED THE CROWN OF LANCRE IN THE PROPS BOX AND HAS PUT IT ON HIS HEAD.

VITOLLER: For goodness sake, laddie. It hardly fits. Put it back.

23. Lancre Castle. Night.

THE FOOL LIES ASLEEP IN A DOORWAY. DUKE FELMET APPEARS. HE GRABS THE FOOL AND HEAVES HIM UPRIGHT.

FOOL: Aaagh.

DUKE FELMET: It's the witches isn't it! They're out there, aren't they!

FOOL: Marry nuncle...

DUKE FELMET: Portents! Strange omens! Short sharp showers of shrimps. Geese walking backwards! They're putting an influence on the land, aren't they!

FOOL: No, my lord. They never...

DUKE FELMET: Who asked you?!?

FOOL: Er... you did my lord.

DUKE FELMET: Are you arguing with me?

FOOL: No, my lord!

DUKE FELMET: I thought so! You're in league with them I suppose?

FOOL: My lord!

DUKE FELMET: You're all in league you people! The whole pack of you! You're nothing but a pack of ringleaders.

THE DUKE GOES ONTO THE BALCONY AND SHOUTS FROM IT.

DUKE FELMET: Do you all hear me? I am the king! *(SOBBING)* I am the king... Gods! I hate this kingdom!

THE FOOL OFFERS THE DUKE HIS HANDKERCHIEF.

DUKE FELMET: Is this a dagger I see before me?

FOOL: Um, no, my lord. It's my handkerchief. You can sort of tell the difference if you look closely. It doesn't have as many sharp edges.

DUKE FELMET: Good Fool. Kneel beside me, Fool.

THE FOOL DOES AS HE IS BID.

DUKE FELMET: Are you loyal, Fool? Are you trustworthy?

FOOL: I swore to follow my lord until death.

DUKE FELMET: I didn't want to. She made me do it. I didn't want...

LADY FELMET APPEARS IN THE DOORWAY.

LADY FELMET: Leonal!

DUKE FELMET: Yes, my dear?

LADY FELMET: What is the meaning of all this?

DUKE FELMET: Witches, I suspect.

FOOL: I really don't think...

LADY FELMET: That is clearly apparent. You are an idiot.

FOOL: A fool, my lady.

LADY FELMET: So. Still they defy you.

DUKE FELMET: How should I fight magic?

FOOL: With words, my lord.

LADY FELMET: What did you say?

FOOL: In the guild we learned that words can be more powerful even than magic.

DUKE FELMET: Clown! Words are just words! Sticks and stones may break my bones – but words can never hurt me.

FOOL: My lord, there are such words that can. Liar. Usurper. Murderer... Such words have no truth. But they can spread like fire underground. Words can fight even witches.

LADY FELMET: What words?

FOOL: Crone. Evil eye. Stupid old woman.

LADY FELMET: You are not entirely a fool, are you. You refer of course to rumour.

DUKE FELMET: Yes. Yes it's the witches. We must tell the world about the witches. They're evil. Evil. Evil...

24. GRANNY W.'S COTTAGE. NIGHT.

GRANNY W. LIES ASLEEP IN BED. THE ROOM SHAKES GENTLY AND GRANNY W. IS IMMEDIATELY AWAKE.

GRANNY W.: Who's there? There's something out there... Something forlorn... something lost...

GRANNY W.'S MIND SEARCH CONTINUES ACROSS THE LAND, AT FIRST SLOWLY, BUT THEN INCREASING IN SPEED.

GRANNY W.: Aaaaagh!

SHE HAS BEEN THROWN OUT OF BED BY THE FORCE OF HER INVESTIGATION.

GRANNY W.: And to think I had expected it to be small!

25. THE STANDING STONE. NIGHT.

GRANNY W. IS SEARCHING THE AREA WITH HER MIND.

GRANNY W.: Who are you? What do you want?

MAGRAT ENTERS.

MAGRAT: You felt it too?

GRANNY W.: I thought it was something small. Small as a vermine.

MAGRAT: Vermine?

GRANNY W.: Furry creature. A more careful relative of the lemming. Only throws itself over small pebbles. Where's Gytha?

MAGRAT TURNS HER GAZE TOWARDS THE TOWN OF LANCRE BELOW THEM.

26. NANNY O.'S COTTAGE. NIGHT.

THE SOUND OF CAROUSING POURS OUT INTO THE STREET. GRANNY W. AND MAGRAT APPEAR.

MAGRAT: Do you think we should have brought a bottle?

GRANNY W.: Sounds to me as if there's a deal too many bottles in there already.

AS THEY ARE ABOUT TO KNOCK AT THE DOOR A MAN COMES OUT, RATHER THE WORSE FOR DRINK.

MAN: Happy Hogswatch night, Missus!

GRANNY W.: Msss.

MAN: I am most frightfully sorry...

GRANNY W.: Come, Magrat.

27. NANNY O.'S COTTAGE. NIGHT.

THE FRONT DOOR OPENS AND GRANNY W. AND MAGRAT ENTER. THEY SQUEEZE THEIR WAY THROUGH THE ASSEMBLED REVELLERS TOWARDS NANNY O. WHO SITS IN HER COMFORTABLE ARMCHAIR BY THE FIRE.

NANNY O.: What ho, my old boiler! See you turned up, then! Have a drink. Have two! Wotcher Magrat.

GRANNY W.: We're not staying. I can see you're busy. We just wondered whether you might have noticed – anything. Tonight. A little while ago.

NANNY O.: Well... *(BRIGHTLY)* Our Darren's eldest was sick. Been at his dad's beer.

GRANNY W.: Unless he was *extremely* ill, I doubt if it was what I was referring to.

NANNY O.: Someone tried to dance on the table. Fell right into our Reet's pumpkin dip! We had a good laugh!

GRANNY W.: I was alluding to things of a *different* nature.

SHE CASTS A CLANDESTINE WINK IN NANNY O.'S DIRECTION.

NANNY O.: Something wrong with your eye, Esme?

GRANNY W.: Extremely worrying developments of a magical tendency are even now afoot. It might be a good idea if we go somewhere more private to talk.

28. NANNY O.'S COTTAGE. NIGHT.

THE THREE WITCHES EMERGE FROM THE COTTAGE TO THE BACK GARDEN AND MAKE FOR THE WASH-HOUSE.

GRANNY W.: It's out there somewhere, in the mountains and the high forests. And it is very big.

MAGRAT: I thought it was looking for some-one. It put me in mind of a dog. You know. Lost. And puzzled.

GRANNY W.: Yes. Something like that. A very *big* dog.

MAGRAT: Worried.

GRANNY W.: Searching.

MAGRAT: Getting angry.

THEY ENTER THE WASH-HOUSE.

29. THE WASH-HOUSE. NIGHT.

NANNY O.: Could be a troll... I left the best part of a pint in there, you know!

GRANNY W.: I know what a troll's mind feels like, Gytha.

NANNY O.: They say there's really big trolls up towards the hub. And ice-giants. And big hairy wossnames that live above the snowline. But you don't mean anything like that, do you.

GRANNY W.: No.

NANNY O.: Oh.

NANNY O. GOES TO THE BIG COPPER IN THE CENTRE OF THE SMALL ROOM AND TAKES THE LID OFF.

NANNY O.: We'd better have a look then.

MAGRAT: What are you going to do?

NANNY O.: I always say you can't go wrong with a good invocation. Haven't done one for years.

MAGRAT: Oh but you can't. Not here. We need a cauldron and a magic sword. And an octogram. And spices, and all sorts of stuff.

GRANNY W.: You don't need none of that. You just use whatever you've got.

SHE LOOKS AROUND AND PICKS UP A LARGE WOODEN SPOON. THEY ALL GATHER ROUND THE COPPER.

GRANNY W.: Ahem. We conjure and abjure thee by means of this long and terrible wooden spoon.

MAGRAT: See how we scatter... rather old washing soda and extremely hard soap flakes in thy honour... Really, Nanny; I don't think...

GRANNY W.: Silence! Now you, Gytha.

NANNY O.: And I invoke and bind thee with the balding scrubbing brush of Art and the washboard of Protection.

THE WATER IN THE COPPER BOILS VIOLENTLY...

EPISODE THREE

1. NANNY O.'S WASH-HOUSE. NIGHT.

THE BOILING WATER FORMS ITSELF INTO THE GIANT AND FEARSOME HEAD OF A DEMON. IT LOOKS AROUND THE ROOM AND FIXES ITS MALEVOLENT GAZE ON THE THREE WITCHES. THE WITCHES REGARD IT WARILY. THE DEMON IS THE FIRST TO BREAK THE SILENCE.

DEMON: Who dares to invoke xxxbbyyyqw?

NANNY O.: Where were you when the vowels were being handed out? Behind the door?

DEMON: You are allowed three questions.

GRANNY W.: Right, is there something strange at large in the kingdom?

DEMON: You mean... stranger than usual?

NANNY O.: Get on with it. My feet are freezing.

MAGRAT: And no lying, otherwise it'll be the scrubbing brush for you.

DEMON: No. There is nothing strange.

GRANNY W.: Humph! Is there something in the kingdom that wasn't there before?

DEMON: No.

GRANNY W.: What the disc's going on?... And no mucking about trying to wriggle out of it, otherwise I'll boil you.

DEMON: I protest at this treatment...

GRANNY W.: Yes. Well, we haven't got time to bandy legs with you all night. Word games might be all right for wizards. We've got other fish to fry.

NANNY O.: Or boil...

DEMON: Look! We're not supposed to volunteer information just like that. You know there are rules.

NANNY O.: There's some old oil in the can on the shelf, Magrat.

DEMON: Look, if I simply tell you...

GRANNY W.: Yes?

DEMON: You won't let on, will you?

GRANNY W.: Not a word.

MAGRAT: Lips are sealed.

DEMON: Ahhh... There is nothing new in the kingdom. But the land has woken up.

GRANNY W.: What do you mean?

DEMON: Oh – it's unhappy. It wants a king that cares for it.

GRANNY W.: You don't mean people do you.

THE DEMON SHAKES HIS HEAD.

GRANNY W.: No. I didn't think so... saw the mind of a whole country!

DEMON: Can I go now?

GRANNY W.: Oh. Yes. Run along.

DEMON: I say, you wouldn't mind banishing me, would you?

GRANNY W.: What?

DEMON: Only I'd feel better for being properly banished. 'Run along' lacks that certain something.

GRANNY W.: Oh, if it gives you pleasure. Magrat.

MAGRAT: Yes?

GRANNY W.: Do the honours, will you?

MAGRAT: Certainly. Right. Um... 'Begone, foul fiend, unto the blackest pit from whence ye came...'

THE WATER IN THE COPPER BOILS ONCE AGAIN AS THE DEMON 'MELTS'.

MAGRAT: Run along hee hee.

THE DEMON DISAPPEARS BENEATH THE WATER.

2. STO PLAIN. DAY.

IT IS WINTER. THE CARTS OF VITOLLER'S TRAVELLING PLAYERS APPEAR.

3. PLAYERS' CART. DAY.

INSIDE THE LAST CART ARE TOMJON AND HWEL.

HWEL: Hoogh!

HWEL HOLDS AN APPLE OUT TO TOMJON.

HWEL: Apple... apple.

TOMJON SMILES BUT SAYS NOTHING.

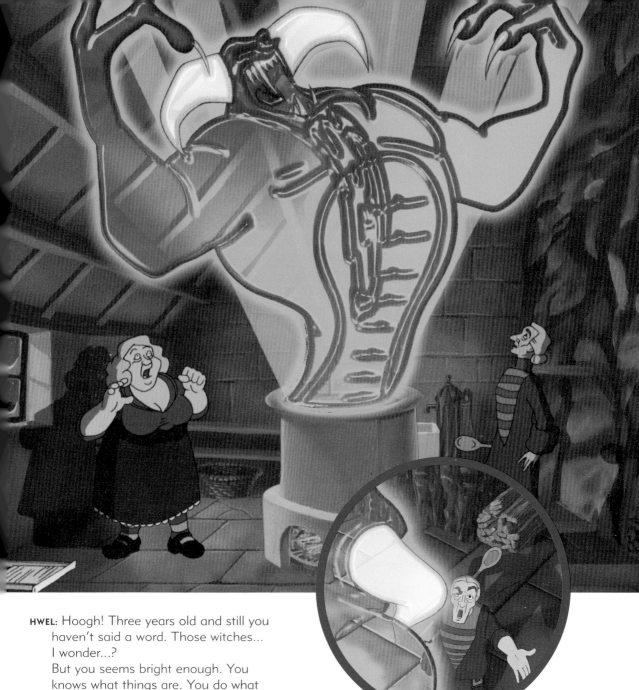

HWEL: Hoogh! Three years old and still you haven't said a word. Those witches... I wonder...?
But you seems bright enough. You knows what things are. You do what you're told... I just wish you'd speak.

NANNY O.: A good memory is what he ought to have, he'll always remember the words...

HER IMAGE FADES.

TOMJON: They say this fruit be like unto the world

So sweet. Or like, say I, the heart of man

So red without and yet within unclue'd,

We find the worm, the rot, the flaw.

However glows his bloom the bite

Proves many a man to be rotten at the core. Ha Ha...

HWEL: He's talking!

4. STO PLAIN. DAY.

HWEL BURSTS OUT OF THE BACK OF THE CART.

HWEL: The boy! He's... he's quoting! You've got to come!

HE RUNS ALONG THE LENGTH OF THE CONVOY TOWARDS THE FOREMOST CART WHERE VITOLLER SITS.

VITOLLER: What ails you?

HWEL: Your son, Tomjon, has declaimed his first word!

5. Nanny O.'s Cottage. Night.

NANNY O.: Who's a clever boy then.

6. Granny W.'s Cottage. Night.

GRANNY W. IS MAKING A POT OF TEA. OUTSIDE IT IS SNOWING.

GRANNY W.: Countries... well, they ain't even *alive* for goodness sake!

SHE MAKES HER WAY TO THE WINDOW.

GRANNY W.: Of course. It'd be a mind made up of all the other little minds inside it; plant minds, bird minds, bear minds, even the great slow minds of the trees themsel...

SHE DRAWS BACK THE CURTAIN.

GRANNY W.: Well.

OUTSIDE IS A HOST OF DISPARATE ANIMALS. WOLVES, BEARS, DEER, RABBITS, WEASELS, BADGERS AND FOXES. THEY ARE ALL STARING AT HER.

7. Granny W.'s Cottage. Evening.

GRANNY W. COMES OUT AND FACES THE ANIMALS. SHE LOOKS AT THEM GRIMLY.

GRANNY W.: I don't know what this spell is, but I'll tell you this for nothing – when it wears off, some of you little beggars had better get moving.

WE SEE VERENCE BEING STABBED AND FALLING DOWN STAIRS.

GRANNY W.: Yes, well, so he killed the old king. That's nature's way, isn't it. You lot know all about this Survival of the woss-name.

8. Outskirts of Lancre. Day.

A TROOP OF SOLDIERS, SOME BEARING BLAZING TORCHES, GALLOP THROUGH A CLEARING IN THE FOREST TOWARDS A SMALL COTTAGE. BESIDE THE COTTAGE, A MAN IS CHOPPING WOOD. THE SERGEANT THROWS HIS TORCH TOWARDS THE THATCHED ROOF.

SERGEANT: Greetings from Duke Felmet!

HE FLINGS A FIRE BRAND.

MAN: Nooo...

GRANNY W.: Anyway, the old king wasn't much of a friend to you, was he? All that hunting and such.

THE FOREST IS BEING CUT DOWN; SOME OF IT IS ON FIRE.

GRANNY W.: All right! So it's selfish. That's what being a witch is all about! Good day to you!

SHE MARCHES BACK TO HER FRONT DOOR AND ENTERS.

THE OTHER SOLDIERS THROW THEIR TORCHES ONTO THE ROOF.

MAN: No! Nooo!

9. LANCRE CASTLE. DAY.

IT IS SPRINGTIME. GREEBO CHASES A SMALL WHITE CAT BY THE CASTLE GATE.

10. LANCRE CASTLE. DAY.

SCARED LADY CAT: Meow!

VERENCE IS IN THE GREAT HALL. GREEBO ENTERS. VERENCE LOOKS AT GREEBO AND CHUCKLES.

VERENCE: Ha ha. What was it he said...?

AS VERENCE THINKS BACK TO WHEN HE FIRST BECAME A GHOST, HE HEARS HIS OWN VOICE FOLLOWED BY THAT OF DEATH.

VERENCE: *(V.O.)* Won't anyone be able to see me?

DEATH: *(V.O.)* Oh, the psychically inclined. And cats of course...

GREEBO: Meow!

VERENCE: Only one type of person would keep a cat like you. A witch.
And if a witch isn't psychically inclined, then I'm a puff of wind! If I could get a witch into the castle... Here pussy, pussy...

GREEBO HISSES AND SPITS AT VERENCE.

VERENCE: Cat. Come on puss, puss. Ah! Tch tch tch...

GREEBO GETS TO HIS FEET AND FOLLOWS VERENCE.

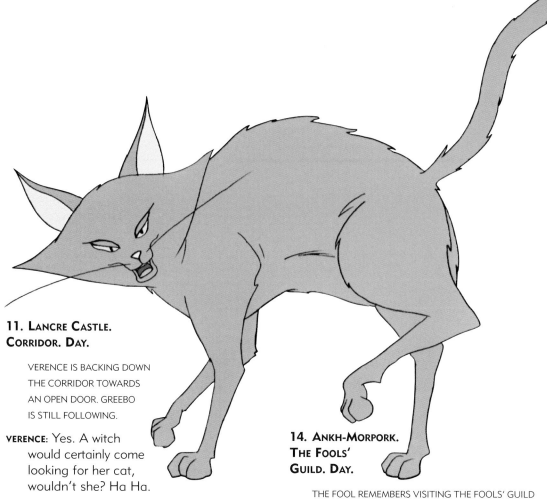

11. LANCRE CASTLE. CORRIDOR. DAY.

VERENCE IS BACKING DOWN THE CORRIDOR TOWARDS AN OPEN DOOR. GREEBO IS STILL FOLLOWING.

VERENCE: Yes. A witch would certainly come looking for her cat, wouldn't she? Ha Ha.

VERENCE GOES THROUGH THE DOORWAY AND GREEBO DOES LIKEWISE.

12. LANCRE CASTLE. LUMBER ROOM. DAY.

THE ROOM INTO WHICH VERENCE HAS ENTICED NANNY O.'S CAT IS FULL OF JUNK.

VERENCE: Here puss, puss, puss... There's plenty of mice and things in here, d'you see? The rain blows in through the broken window. And there's all these tapestries to sleep on.

VERENCE TURNS HIS ATTENTIONS TO THE DOOR. IT BEGINS TO MOVE AND THEN SLAMS SHUT.

VERENCE: Sorry about that.

HE WALKS THROUGH THE DOOR.

13. MEADOW NEAR THE CASTLE. DAY.

THE FOOL IS LYING ON HIS STOMACH, STARING INTO A SMALL LAKE.

FOOL: I suppose somewhere on the disc there must be someone more miserable than me. I didn't ask to be a fool. Huh. It wouldn't have mattered if I had.

14. ANKH-MORPORK. THE FOOLS' GUILD. DAY.

THE FOOL REMEMBERS VISITING THE FOOLS' GUILD IN HIS YOUTH, WITH HIS GRANDFATHER. AN ANCIENT FOOL APPROACHED WHEN THEY RANG FOR ADMITTANCE.

FOOLS: *(CHANTING)* Hast thy seeneth my Mother-in-Law

I'm not saying she is fat,

but when she beneth over,

there occureth an eclips in Lancre.

GRANDFATHER: You will learn, my lad, in the years to come that there is nothing more serious than jesting. The Fools' Guild will knock some nonsense into you.

RINGS THE BELL.

YOUNG FOOL: Yes, Grandad.

GRANDFATHER: It runs in the family, you know. I won the honorary cap and bells of the Grand Prix des Idiots Blithering four years in a row! And your Father was credited with seven official New Jokes.

YOUNG FOOL: Yes, Grandad.

THE VENERABLE AND ANCIENT FOOL HAS REACHED THE GATES AND PULLED THEM OPEN. HE LOOKS DOWN AT THE YOUNG FOOL.

ANCIENT FOOL: This the lad?

GRANDFATHER: Indeed, your absurdity.

ANCIENT FOOL: Well? What have you got to say for yourself?

YOUNG FOOL: Marry, sire. Prithee. What do you get if you cross a duck and a robin? A Christmas Quacker. Ha Ha.

GRANDFATHER LOOKS APOLOGETICALLY AT THE ANCIENT FOOL.

GRANDFATHER: I'm sorry, your absurdity.

THE ANCIENT FOOL GLOWERS AT THE YOUNG FOOL.

ANCIENT FOOL: You will never, never ever utter a joke that has not been approved by the Guild! Who are you to decide what is amusing. You have much to learn. The three hundred and eighty-three Guild-approved jokes in the 'Monster Book of Fun'; and the glossary, which is much, much longer...

HE GRABS THE YOUNG FOOL BY THE EAR.

ANCIENT FOOL: Come, boy. We'll make a fool of you yet.

HE DRAGS HIM INTO THE QUADRANGLE BY HIS EAR.

FOOLS: *(CHANTING)* Marry – There were these three fellows in ye Mended Drum
– A troll, a dwarf and a human.

15. MEADOW NEAR CASTLE. DAY.

THE FOOL IS BROUGHT BACK TO THE PRESENT BY THE SOUND OF SINGING.

HE SEES MAGRAT WALKING THROUGH THE MEADOW, PICKING FLOWERS.

MAGRAT: La la la la... Here's Woolly Felwort. And Treacle.
Wormseed, which is for inflammation of the ears. La la la...
And Five-leaved False Mandrake, sovereign against fluxes of the bladder... ah!
And Old Man's Frogbit. That's for constipation.

THE FOOL AND MAGRAT SEE EACH OTHER.

FOOL: Er...

MAGRAT: Hallo...

FOOL: Whoops!

> HE STARTS TO RUN BACK TO THE CASTLE.

MAGRAT: Don't...

> MAGRAT LOOKS AFTER HIS DEPARTING FIGURE.

MAGRAT: Oh bugger.

16. VILLAGE IN LANCRE. DAY.

> A GROUP OF SOLDIERS RIDE THROUGH, SETTING FIRE TO COTTAGES AND CUTTING DOWN THE VILLAGERS.

SERGEANT: Compliments of Duke Felmet!

DUKE FELMET: Ha Ha Ha.

17. OPEN LAND BY THE STANDING STONE. NIGHT.

> THE THREE WITCHES ARE STANDING BY THEIR CAULDRON.

NANNY O.: Greebo hasn't been home for two days. I can't find him anywhere. It's not like him.

GRANNY W.: 'Course it's like him. He's a fat, cunning, evil-smelling, multiple rapist. Anyway, cats can look after themselves. Countries can't... I have intelligence to report. Light the fire, Magrat.

MAGRAT: Hmmmn? Oh. Yes.

> MAGRAT WANDERS ABSENT-MINDEDLY ACROSS THE MOORLAND PICKING UP SMALL TWIGS.

NANNY O.: Doesn't seem to be her normal self.

GRANNY W.: No. Could be an improvement.

NANNY O.: Something on your mind, Esme.

GRANNY W.: The kingdom is worried.

NANNY O.: Yes. All this taxing and killing folk. Felmet hates the kingdom.

GRANNY W.: I didn't mean the people. I meant the kingdom.

NANNY O.: It wants a better king. Is that it?

GRANNY W.: No! That is, yes. Look. It doesn't have the same kind of likes and dislikes as people, right?

NANNY O.: Well, it wouldn't, would it.

GRANNY W.: But it expects the king to care for it. Felmet just wants the power. He hates the kingdom.

NANNY O.: What are we going to do about it?

GRANNY W.: Nothing. You know we can't meddle.

NANNY O.: You saved that baby.

GRANNY W.: That's not meddling.

NANNY O.:
Have it your way. But maybe one day he'll return. Destiny you know. And you said we should hide the crown. It'll all come back, you mark my words. Hurry up with that tea, Magrat.

MAGRAT BUSIES HERSELF WITH THE FIRE.

MAGRAT: You know the Fool who lives up at the castle?

NANNY O.: Little man with runny eyes?

MAGRAT: Not that little... What's his name, do you happen to know?

GRANNY W.: He's just called Fool. No job for a man, that. Running around with bells on.

NANNY O.: His mother was a beldame, from over Blackglass way. Bit of a beauty when she was younger. Broke many a heart, she did. Bit of a scandal there, I did hear.

GRANNY W.: Why do you want to know, Magrat?

MAGRAT: Oh... One of the girls in the village was asking me...

NANNY O.: It's a steady job, I'll give you that. Hee Hee.

GRANNY W. & NANNY O.: *(STIFLE GIGGLES)*

MAGRAT: You're a pair of silly old women. And I'm going home!

SHE STANDS UP AND STALKS OFF.

NANNY O.: Well!

GRANNY W.: You haven't been putting ideas in her head, have you?

NANNY O.: What do you mean?

GRANNY W.: You know what I mean.

NANNY O.: Just like when you were a gel. Stuck up, you were.

GRANNY W.: At least I spent most of the time upright! You were the talk of the whole village!

NANNY O.: And you were too! Called you the 'Ice-Maiden'!

GRANNY W.: I wouldn't sully my lips with sayin' what they called you!

NANNY O.: Oh yes? Well, let me tell you, my good woman...

GRANNY W.: Don't you dare talk to me in that tone of voice! I'm not anyone's good woman.

NANNY O.: Right!

GRANNY W.: I should have known better than to listen to Magrat. This coven business is ridiculous. Attracts entirely the wrong sort of people.

NANNY O.: I'm really glad we had this little talk. Cleared the air.

GRANNY W.: Anyway I really don't have time for all this. I have far more important things to do.

NANNY O.: And me!

GRANNY W.: Goodnight to you.

NANNY O.: And you!

THEY MARCH STIFFLY AWAY FROM EACH OTHER IN OPPOSITE DIRECTIONS.

18. MAGRAT'S COTTAGE. NIGHT.

MAGRAT ENTERS AND BEGINS LOOKING THROUGH A LARGE BOOK.

MAGRAT: Love spells... Ah! Oh.
First, I've got to find out your name.

SHE THROWS A STRIP OF APPLE PEEL OVER HER SHOULDER AND SMILES AT THE LETTERS IT FORMS.

MAGRAT: Who'd have thought it? 'Gather ye ferns in a silk handkerchief the first light of dawn...'

19. LANCRE CASTLE. DAWN.

SHAWN STANDS GUARD OUTSIDE THE CASTLE GATE. NANNY O. ARRIVES.

SHAWN: Morning, Mum.

NANNY O.: Morning, our Shawn.

SHAWN: What you doin' up here Mum? If the Duke...

NANNY O.: I've come for Greebo.

SHAWN: Greebo? But he ain't up here, Mum.

NANNY O.: Oh yes he is.

SHE SNIFFS.

NANNY O.: Smell that?

SHAWN SNIFFS THE AIR.

SHAWN: Phwoarr!

NANNY O. WALKS PAST HIM AND THROUGH THE GATES.

MAGRAT: Ooooowooch!

SHE IS IN THE DITCH.

MAGRAT: Somehow when you read these spells, you always think of a bright sunny morning in spring.

MAGRAT TRIES TO PULL HERSELF OUT AND GETS SOAKED BY RAINWATER FROM A BRANCH.

MAGRAT: Waagh!... Oh!

SHE TRIES AGAIN, THIS TIME WITH GREATER SUCCESS.

MAGRAT: Oooh!

NANNY O. IS STRIDING ACROSS THE COURTYARD. BEHIND A WINDOW, DUKE FELMET WATCHES THE WITCH. HE LOOKS WORRIED.

DUKE FELMET: A witch! And she's coming to get me!

20. EDGE OF THE FOREST. EARLY MORNING.

MAGRAT SEES SHAWN APPROACHING IN HASTE.

SHAWN: Is that you, Mss Magrat? It's mam.

MAGRAT: What's happened to her?

SHAWN: She came to the castle to look for Greebo and *the Duke* locked her up. Said she was coming to poison him! And I can't get down to the dungeons to see

her because there's all new guards! They say she's been put in chains – and that means something horrible's going to happen.

MAGRAT: Where were you going?

SHAWN: To fetch our Jason and our Wayne and our Darren and our...

MAGRAT: Wait a moment.

SHAWN: Oh, Mss Magrat! Suppose they try and torture her? You know what she's like when she loses her temper. We'll never hear the last of it, miz.

MAGRAT: Look. Just shut up a minute will you Shawn?

SHAWN: When our Jason finds out, he's going to give the Duke a real seeing to, miz.

MAGRAT: Don't tell him yet. There could be another way.

SHAWN: I'll go and find Granny Weatherwax, shall I, miz? *She'll* know what to do. She's a witch. She'll...

MAGRAT LOOKS DAGGERS AT SHAWN.

SHAWN: Ooops. Um. I didn't mean... You... Well... Um...

MAGRAT: If you happen to see Granny Weatherwax, you can tell her that I will sort it all out. Now go away before I turn you into a frog. You look like one anyway.

21. LANCRE CASTLE. DUNGEON. DAY.

NANNY O. IS IMPRISONED IN STOCKS. THE DUKE AND LADY FELMET STAND NEARBY.

DUKE FELMET: Quite comfortable are we?

NANNY O.: Apart from these stocks, you mean?

DUKE FELMET: I am impervious to your foul blandishments. I scorn your devious wiles. You are to be tortured, I'll have you know.

LADY FELMET: And then... you will be burned!

NANNY O.: Oh Goody!

DUKE FELMET: Oh Goody!

NANNY O.: Well, it's freezing down here. What's that big wardrobe thing with spikes?

DUKE FELMET: Aha! Now you realise, eh? That, my dear lady, is an Iron Maiden. It's the latest thing. Well may you...

NANNY O.: Can I have a go in it?

DUKE FELMET: Your pleas fall on deaf... ears.

LADY FELMET: This insouciance gives you pleasure. But soon you will laugh on the other side of your face!

NANNY O.: It's only got this side.

LADY FELMET: We shall see.

DUKE FELMET: And you need not think any others of your people will come to your aid. We alone hold the keys to this dungeon. Ha ha. You will be an example to all those who have been spreading malicious rumours about me. Do not protest your innocence! I hear the voices all the time, lying...

56

LADY FELMET BEGINS TO DRAG THE DUKE AWAY.

LADY FELMET: Enough.

DUKE FELMET: The faces.

LADY FELMET: Come Leonal.

DUKE FELMET: The wicked lies.

LADY FELMET: We will let her reflect upon her fate for a while.

DUKE FELMET: I wasn't there, and anyway he fell. My porridge – all salty.

THE DOOR SLAMS AND NANNY O. IS LEFT ALONE.

22. Granny W.'s Cottage. Morning.

GRANNY W. STANDS IN THE DOORWAY OF HER COTTAGE IN CONFERENCE WITH SHAWN.

GRANNY W.: You've been a good boy.

SHAWN: Yes'm.

GRANNY W.: Was there something else?

SHAWN: It's not true what everyone's been saying about our mam, is it m'm? She doesn't go round putting evil curses on folk.

GRANNY W.: Well, your mam does upset people sometimes.

SHAWN: Yes. But they've been saying terrible things about you, too m'm, saving your presence, m'm.

GRANNY W.'S EYES BLAZE.

GRANNY W.: What things?

SHAWN: *(MUMBLES)* Don't like to say, m'm.

GRANNY W.: *(FIERCELY)* What things?

SHAWN: A lot of things that aren't true. Like, old Verence was a bad king and you helped him on the throne, and you caused that bad winter the other year, and Old Norbert's cow din't give no milk after you looked at it... Lot of lies, m'm.

GRANNY W.: Right!

SHE SLAMS THE DOOR BUT THEN PEERS OUT AGAIN.

GRANNY W.: Who's Old Norbert?

23. LANCRE CASTLE. DUNGEON. DAY.

NANNY O. IS STILL SITTING IN THE STOCKS.

NANNY O.: All right. I can see you.

VERENCE COMES INTO VIEW.

NANNY O.: 'Ere. I know you. You're dead.

VERENCE: I prefer the term 'passed over'.

NANNY O.: You haven't seen a cat around here have you?

VERENCE: Yes. He's in a room upstairs, asleep.

NANNY O.: That's all right then. I was beginning to worry.

VERENCE: I fear, madam, that I may be responsible for your present predicament. I wished to attract a witch.

NANNY O.: I suppose you're no good at locks?

VERENCE: I fear they would be beyond my feeble capabilities as yet. But surely, to a witch, all this is so much...

NANNY O.: Solid iron. You might be able to walk through it, but I can't.

24. MAGRAT'S COTTAGE. DAY.

MAGRAT COMES OUT OF HER COTTAGE CARRYING A BAG OF APPLES. SHE TAKES A BREAD-KNIFE OUT OF THE BASKET AND STUDIES IT.

MAGRAT: Yes. A good sharp bread-knife. That's probably the best friend a girl... a *woman* could have.

SHE BEGINS TO MAKE HER WAY TO THE CASTLE.

25. LANCRE CASTLE. DUNGEON. DAY.

NANNY O. AND VERENCE ARE PLAYING I-SPY.

NANNY O.: I-spy with my little eye something beginning with P.

VERENCE: Hoogh! Pliers.

NANNY O.: No.

VERENCE: Pilliwinks.

NANNY O.: That's a pretty name. What is it?

VERENCE: It's a kind of thumbscrew. Look.

NANNY O.: It's not that.

VERENCE: Erm... Smouldering Boot of Punishment?

NANNY O.: You're a bit too good with the names of these things. You sure you didn't use them when you were alive?

VERENCE: Absolutely, nanny!

NANNY O.: Boys that tell lies go to a bad place.

VERENCE: Lady Felmet had most of them installed herself. It's the truth!

NANNY O.: Right then. It was 'pinchers'.

VERENCE: But pinchers is another name for pliers.

26. LANCRE CASTLE. DAY.

A CROWD HAS GATHERED OUTSIDE THE GATES OF THE CASTLE.

GRANNY WEATHERWAX APPROACHES, A BASKET OF APPLES OVER HER ARM. SHE STOPS WHEN SHE SEES THE CROWD. A MAN WHISPERS TO HER.

MAN: There's a witch in the dungeons. And foul tortures they say.

GRANNY W.: Nonsense!

THE MAN RECOGNISES HER AND BLANCHES.

GRANNY W.: I expect she's just gone to advise the king or something.

GRANNY W. ADDRESSES THE CROWD.

GRANNY W.: I suggest you all return home. There has probably been a misunderstanding. Everyone knows that a witch cannot be held against her will.

SHE BEGINS TO WALK TOWARDS THE CASTLE GATES. THE CROWD PARTS TO LET HER THROUGH.

GRANNY W. REACHES THE CASTLE GATES. TWO GUARDS STAND IN HER WAY. SHE STARES HARD AT GUARD 1.

GRANNY W.: I am a harmless old seller of apples. Pray let me past, dearie.

GUARD 1: No-one must enter the castle. Orders of the Duke.

GRANNY W.: I know you, Champott Poldy.

GUARD 1 TREMBLES.

GUARD 1: Ohhhh.

GRANNY W.: Don't worry about it. Have an apple.

GUARD 2 STEPS FORWARD.

GUARD 2: So that's witches' magic, is it? Maybe it frightens these country idiots, woman, but it doesn't frighten me.

GRANNY W. REARRANGES HER HAT.

GRANNY W.: You must be one of these here new-fangled mercenaries the Duke's brung in. I imagine it takes a lot to frighten a big strong lad like you.

GUARD 2: Old ladies like you. Twisting people around. It shouldn't be stood for.

GRANNY W.: Just as you like.

SHE PUSHES HIS SPEAR TO ONE SIDE. HE GRABS HER SHOULDER ROUGHLY.

GUARD 2: Listen. I *said*...

GRANNY W. PIERCES HIS FOREARM WITH A HATPIN. HE DROPS THE SPEAR.

GUARD 2: Owooooch!

GRANNY W. RUNS PAST HIM AND INTO THE CASTLE.

27. LANCRE CASTLE. DUNGEON. DAY.

DUKE AND LADY FELMET STAND OVER NANNY OGG. THE FOOL STANDS NEARBY.

LADY FELMET: We shall begin with the showing of the implements.

NANNY O.: Seen 'em. Leastways, all the ones beginning with P, S, I, T and W.

LADY FELMET: Then let us see how long you can keep that light conversational tone. Light the brazier, Felmet.

DUKE FELMET: Light the brazier, Fool.

THE FOOL GOES TOWARDS THE BRAZIER AND TAKES SOME MATCHES.

FOOL: I don't like doing this, you know.

NANNY O.: Fine. I'll remember that you didn't like it.

DUKE FELMET: What's that?

NANNY O.: Nothing.

VERENCE BLOWS OUT THE FOOL'S MATCH.

NANNY O.: Is this going to take long? Only I haven't had me breakfast yet.

EVERY TIME THE FOOL LIGHTS A MATCH, IT IS BLOWN OUT BY SOMEONE INVISIBLE.

LADY FELMET: Hurry up, man!

FOOL: Doesn't seem to want to light...

THE DUKE CUFFS THE FOOL ROUND THE EAR.

DUKE FELMET: Infirm of purpose! Weak!

FOOL: Ow!

DUKE FELMET: And give me the box! Go outside and see that we are not disturbed!

THE FOOL RUNS OUT OF THE DUNGEON.

28. LANCRE CASTLE. DAY.

GUARD 1 HAS BEEN LEFT ON GATE DUTY ALONE. MAGRAT IS CONFRONTING HIM.

GUARD 1: What?

MAGRAT: I *said* I've come to sell my lovely apples. Don't you listen?

GUARD 1: You're not a witch, are you?

MAGRAT: Of course not! Do I look like one.

GUARD 1: Right. Pass apple-seller.

MAGRAT: Thank you.

SHE EXITS.

29. LANCRE CASTLE. GREAT HALL. DAY.

TWO GUARDS STAND AT THE FOOT OF THE STAIR-CASE. MAGRAT ENTERS.

GUARD 2: Well, well. Come to keep us company, have you, my pretty?

GUARD 2 IS JOINED BY HIS COLLEAGUE.

MAGRAT: I was looking for the dungeons.

GUARD 3: Just fancy. I reckon we can help you out then.

GUARD 2: *(LAUGHS)*

THE TWO GUARDS ESCORT MAGRAT OUT OF THE ROOM.

30. Lancre Castle. Dungeon. Day.

NANNY OGG SITS IN THE STOCKS. LADY FELMET
DRAWS A PAIR OF RED-HOT PLIERS FROM THE
BRAZIER.

LADY FELMET: And now we will commence...

31. Lancre Castle. Corridor. Day.

OUTSIDE THE DUNGEON, THE TWO GUARDS ARE
FROGMARCHING MAGRAT ALONG.

MAGRAT: I should warn you. I am not, as I
may appear, a simple apple-seller.

GUARD 2: Well fancy that.

MAGRAT: I am, in fact, a witch.

GUARD 3: Fair enough. I've always wondered
what it would be like to kiss a witch.
Around here they do say you gets
turned into a frog. If you kiss a witch.

GUARD 2: I reckon then... heh heh heh; you
kissed one years ago. Ha ha ha ha ha!

HE THROWS MAGRAT AGAINST THE WALL. THE TWO
GUARDS PIN HER THERE.

1. LANCRE CASTLE. CORRIDOR. DAY.

DUKE FELMET: *(O.O.S.)* Aaaaaaaaaghh!

2. LANCRE CASTLE. CORRIDOR. DAY.

THE TWO GUARDS HAVE MAGRAT PINNED AGAINST THE UNEVEN STONE WALL OF THE CORRIDOR. THEY ARE LEERING HORRIBLY AT HER, THEIR INTENT QUITE OBVIOUS, EVEN TO MAGRAT WHO, AS WE KNOW, IS A STRANGER TO MATTERS OF THE FLESH. SHE STRUGGLES VAINLY WITH HER TWO CAPTORS. THE HYSTERICAL DUKE FELMET CONTINUES TO SCREAM.

DUKE FELMET: *(O.O.S.)* Aaaaaaaaaghhhh!

GUARD 3: That's a witch having it the hard way. Do yourself a favour.

GUARD 2.: You got to tie her hands and gag her. They can't do no magic if they can't speak or wave their hands about.

FOOL: *(O.O.S.)* You can take your hands off her!

GUARD 2.: This is a witch we have here. So you can go and tinkle somewhere else.

MAGRAT STRUGGLES.

GUARD 2.: I like a girl with spirit.

THE FOOL ADVANCES TOWARDS THE GROUP.

FOOL: I told you to let her go.

MAGRAT KNOCKS OUT GUARD 3 AND PREVENTS GUARD 2 FROM KILLING THE FOOL BY HOLDING HER KNIFE AT HIS THROAT.

MAGRAT: Let go of him. *(PAUSES)* You're wondering whether I really would cut your throat. I don't know either. Think of the fun we could have finding out.

MAGRAT IS DISTRACTED BY A SCREAM FROM THE TORTURE CHAMBER AND THE GUARD RUNS OFF.

DUKE FELMET: *(O.O.S.)* Ahhhhhh.

FOOL: They've got her in the torture chamber and I don't like the sound of it. It's going too far. I couldn't get in and I came to look for someone...

MAGRAT: Well, you found me.

SHE BEGINS TO WALK DOWN THE CORRIDOR. THE FOOL FOLLOWS.

FOOL: The door's locked. There's all sorts of noises but the door's locked.

MAGRAT: Well, it's a dungeon, isn't it?

FOOL: They're not supposed to lock it from the inside.

MAGRAT HAS REACHED THE DUNGEON. SHE TRIES THE DOOR. IT IS LOCKED. SHE RUNS HER HANDS OVER THE DOOR'S SURFACE.

DUKE FELMET: *(O.O.S.)* Ahhhh.

FOOL: They said you were a witch. Are you really? You don't look like a witch, you look very... that is... not like a, you know, crone at all, but... you're beautiful.

MAGRAT: You'd better stand back, Verence. I'm not sure how this is going to work.

FOOL: How did you know my name?

MAGRAT IS NOW CONCENTRATING ON THE DOOR, HOLDING BOTH PALMS AGAINST IT.

MAGRAT: Oh, I expect I heard it somewhere...

FOOL: I shouldn't think so. I never use it. I mean, it's not a popular name with the duke. It was me mam, you see. They like to name you after kings, I suppose, and...

MAGRAT SCREAMS AND REELS BACK FROM THE DOOR. THE FOOL CATCHES HER AS SHE FALLS.

A KNOT IN THE TIMBER OF THE DOOR SEEMS TO GROW, THEN A GREEN SHOOT SPROUTS FROM IT. THIS IS FOLLOWED BY ANOTHER, THEN ANOTHER...

A ROOT SHOOTS OUT, FOLLOWED BY ANOTHER.

MAGRAT: Run!

THE DOOR BURSTS INTO BLOOM AND THE DUNGEON OPENS UNDERS ITS PRESSURE.

MAGRAT: I think I gave it rather a lot.

GRANNY W. EMERGES FROM THE SHADOWS.

GRANNY W.: I reckon you did! Come on. We'd better see what she's been getting up to.

THE TWO WITCHES AND THE FOOL ARRIVE AT WHAT USED TO BE THE DUNGEON DOOR AND BEGIN TO CLAMBER AROUND THE NEW ROOTS AND BRANCHES.

GRANNY W.: I wouldn't have done it like that. I'd have tried the stones if it had been me. Not that I'm objecting, mind you.

MAGRAT: I can't do stones.

GRANNY W.: Well, no. Rocks is an acquired taste.

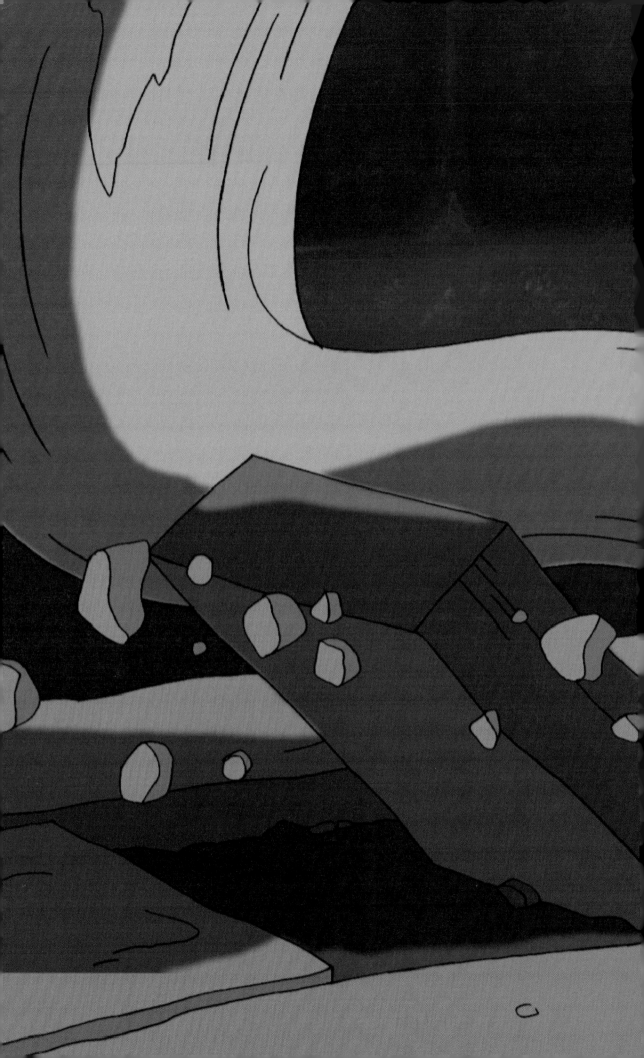

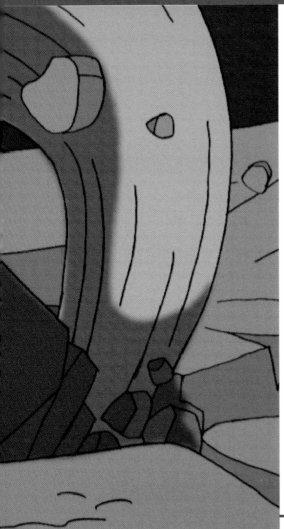

3. LANCRE CASTLE. DUNGEON. DAY.

NANNY OGG IS STILL SITTING IN THE STOCKS,
WATCHING DUKE FELMET.

FELMET SCREAMS.

HE IS ON HIS HANDS AND KNEES. A DAGGER HANGS
IN FRONT OF HIM. LADY FELMET IS CROUCHED NEAR
THE DESTRUCTION OF THE DOORWAY. GRANNY W.
AND MAGRAT APPEAR THROUGH THE GREENERY.

NANNY O.: You took your time. Let me out of
this, will you? I'm getting cramp!

GRANNY W. AND MAGRAT CROSS TO NANNY O.,
PAST THE HOVERING KNIFE WHICH SPINS IN THE AIR
IN FRONT OF DUKE FELMET AND IS THEN THRUST
TOWARDS HIM. HE SCREAMS.

DUKE FELMET: Aaaargh!

AS MAGRAT RESCUES NANNY O. FROM THE STOCKS,
THE LATTER NODS IN THE KNIFE'S DIRECTION.

NANNY O.: He's doing well, isn't he.

MAGRAT: Can they see him?

NANNY O.: Shouldn't think so.

THE KNIFE FALLS FROM MID-AIR TO THE GROUND.

VERENCE: Oh damn!

GRANNY W. QUICKLY PUTS HER FOOT ON THE KNIFE
AND ADDRESSES THE SPACE OCCUPIED BY VERENCE.

GRANNY W.: The dead shouldn't kill the living. It could be a dangerous wossname. Precedent. We'd all be outnumbered for one thing.

LADY FELMET: Guards! Fool, fetch the guards!

GRANNY W.: They're busy. We were just leaving anyway.

SHE STUDIES THE TWO FELMETS.

GRANNY W.: Which one of you is in charge?

DUKE FELMET GIGGLES.

GRANNY W.: It would be better for you if you left this country. Abdicate or whatever.

LADY FELMET: In favour of whom? A witch? Did you think a bit of simple conjuring would frighten us? We rule by right of conquest. If you defeat us by magic, magic will rule. And that which magic rules, magic destroys. It would destroy you too. You know that. Ha ha. You could strike us down. And perhaps you could find one to replace us. But he would have to be a fool indeed, because he'd know he ruled with your permission. And that would make him no king at all. Is this not true?

GRANNY W.: Yes. It is true... But there is one who could defeat you.

DUKE FELMET: Ahh. The boy? I have many years to prepare. Let him come when he is grown.

4. SCROTE. DAY.

VITOLLER'S TRAVELLING PLAYERS HAVE SET UP THEIR
STAGE AND ARE PERFORMING 'PLEASE YOURSELF'.

BABY TOMJON: He is not dead, I say, who lies beneath this stone,

For whomsoever lives here in my heart

Lives still. And lives forever in this flesh-made throne

Lives; until from this mortal world I too must part.

WILD APPLAUSE.

TOMJON TAKES A BOW. HWEL, VITOLLER AND MRS
VITOLLER ARE WATCHING.

HWEL: By all the gods. I must have been on damn good form when I wrote that!

VITOLLER: Your people know all about magic. What do you make of it?

HWEL: He's spent all his time around the stage, master. It's only natural he should pick things up.

VITOLLER: Do you really believe that?

HWEL: Who knows where such things come from. And who knows what witches may achieve?

VITOLLER LOOKS AT TOMJON.

VITOLLER: He deserves better than this. He shouldn't be standing knee deep in slush in the middle of these forsaken fields with nothing but liberated cabbage for tea. He deserves more. And he shall have it, by the Gods! He shall have it!

5. Lancre Castle. Corridor outside the Dungeon. Day.

GRANNY W. IS MARCHING UP THE CORRIDOR
FOLLOWED BY NANNY O.

NANNY O.: You could give him boils or something... Haemorrhoids are good. It won't stop him ruling, it just means he'll have to rule standing up...

GRANNY W.: Oh I ain't going to give him the pleasure of saying it, but he's got us beaten.

GRANNY W. WALKS ON. NANNY O. PICKS UP AN EGG-
SHAPED STONE FROM THE FLOOR AND PUTS IT IN
HER POCKET. SHE CONTINUES AFTER GRANNY W.
MAGRAT, A LITTLE WAY BEHIND THE OTHER TWO, IS
IN CONVERSATION WITH THE FOOL.

FOOL: Can I see you again?

MAGRAT: Well... I don't know...

FOOL: How about tonight?

MAGRAT: Oh no. I'm very busy tonight.

FOOL: Tomorrow night then?

MAGRAT: I think I should be washing my hair.

FOOL: Or I could get Friday night free.

MAGRAT: We do a lot of work at night, you see...

FOOL: The afternoon then.

MAGRAT: Well...

FOOL: About two o'clock. In the meadow by the pond, all right?

MAGRAT: Well...

FOOL: See you there then. All right?

LADY FELMET: *(O.O.S.)* Fool!

FOOL: I've got to go. The meadow, okay? I'll wear something so you recognise me. All right?

MAGRAT: All right.

6. Lancre Castle. Day.

A LARGE CROWD IS GATHERED OUTSIDE THE CASTLE,
COMPLAINING ABOUT DUKE AND LADY FELMET.
DIBBLER IS SELLING SAUSAGES IN A BUN FROM A
STALL. A MAN IS GRUMBLING ABOUT DIBBLER'S
PRICES.

MAN: Five copper pieces for a sausage in a bun?!?

DIBBLER: There's the transport, fuel, over-heads, etcetera; I'm cuttin' me own throat...

NANNY O., MAGRAT AND GRANNY W. ARRIVE AT THE MAIN DOOR OF THE KEEP.

NANNY O.: Oooh look! There's our Jason! And Wayne; and Darren and Kev and Trev and Nev...

DUKE FELMET APPEARS SILENTLY BEHIND THEM.

DUKE FELMET: Thank you. I will remember their faces.

THE WITCHES TURN SHARPLY TO FACE THE NEW ARRIVAL.

DUKE FELMET: Do you see my archers on the walls?

GRANNY W.: *(O.O.S.)* I see 'em.

DUKE FELMET: *(O.O.S.)* Then smile and wave, so that the people may know that all is well.

NANNY O. OBEYS.

DUKE FELMET: After all, have you not been to see me today on matters of state? I'm not an unreasonable man, I hope. Perhaps if you persuade the people to be calm, I may be prevailed upon to moderate my rule somewhat. I make no promises of course.

NANNY O. CONTINUES TO WAVE FRANTICALLY AT THE CROWD.

NANNY O.: Coo-ee!

GRANNY W.: Will you shut up, you daft old besom! And pull yourself together.

NANNY O.: But there's our Reet and our Sharlene and their babbies. Coo-ee!

THE DUKE STEPS FORWARD AND RAISES A HAND TO STILL THE CROWD.

DUKE FELMET: People of Lancre! Do not be afeared! I will protect you from the witches! They have agreed to leave you in peace! I'll now call upon the respected Granny Weatherwax to say a few words.

GRANNY W.: You've gone a long way too far.

DUKE FELMET: Ha Ha. I have, haven't I!

AT HIS URGING GRANNY W. ADDRESSES THE CROWD.

GRANNY W.: Go home. Come, Gytha... Will you stop waving at people.

THE WITCHES DEPART.

DUKE FELMET: Go then. Get back to your cauldrons wyrd sisters. Ha Ha Ha Ha.

7. THE FOREST. DAY.

THE WITCHES APPEAR. GRANNY W. SITS DOWN ON A TREE-TRUNK AND BURIES HER FACE IN HER HANDS.

MAGRAT: Don't despair. You handled it very well, we thought.

GRANNY W.: I ain't despairing. I'm thinking. Go away.

MAGRAT: Are you all right? They didn't do anything, did they?

NANNY O.: Never laid a finger on me. They're not your real royalty. Old King Grunewald for one. He wouldn't have wasted time waving things around and menacing people. It would have been bang; needles right under the fingernails from the word go and no messing. I... Ahh, I see you've got a follower.

MAGRAT: Sorry?

NANNY O.: The young fellow with the bells. Face like a spaniel what's just been kicked.

MAGRAT: Oh, him. He just follows me around.

NANNY O.: Ooooh. Can be difficult, can that.

MAGRAT: Besides he's so small. And he *capers* all over the place.

NANNY O.: Looked at him carefully, have you?

MAGRAT: Pardon?

NANNY O.: You haven't have you. I thought not. He's a very clever man, that Fool. He ought to have been one of those actor men.

MAGRAT: What do you mean?

NANNY O.: Next time, you have a look at him like a witch. Not like a woman. Good bit of work with the door back there. Coming on well you are. I hope you told him about Greebo.

MAGRAT: He said he'd let him out directly, Nanny.

8. LANCRE CASTLE. DAY.

BY THE CASTLE GATES TWO GUARDS KEEP WATCH. THE FOOL, WITH GREEBO STILL ATTACHED TO HIS HEAD, WALKS OUT OF THE CASTLE AND PAST THE GUARDS.

FOOL: Alright?

GUARD 4: Man just walked past with a cat on his head.

9. THE FOREST. DAY.

THE THREE WITCHES ARE STILL SITTING ON THE FELLED TREE. MAGRAT AND NANNY O. ARE IN CONVERSATION. MAGRAT LOOKS OVER TO GRANNY W.

MAGRAT: She's very upset, isn't she.

NANNY O.: Ah, well. There's the problem, see. The more you gets used to magic, the more you don't want to use it. When you get along in the Craft, you learn that the hardest magic is the sort you don't use at all.

MAGRAT: This isn't some kind of Zen, is it?

NANNY O.: Dunno. Never seen one.

MAGRAT: When we were in the dungeon, Granny said something about trying the rocks. I've never done that, is it hard?

NANNY O.: Ooh, not really. You just prod their memories. You know, of the old days. When they were hot and runny...

SHE REACHES DOWN INTO HER SKIRT.

NANNY O.: Oooooh – That reminds me—

SHE TAKES THE ROCK OUT AND HOLDS IT IN HER HAND, ADDRESSING IT.

NANNY O.: You can come out now.

THE FAINT FORM OF VERENCE BECOMES VISIBLE. NANNY O. CALLS TO GRANNY W.

NANNY O.: Esme? There's someone to see you.

GRANNY W. LIFTS HER HEAD AND LOOKS OVER TO THE BARELY VISIBLE FORM OF VERENCE. VERENCE BOWS GRACIOUSLY TOWARDS GRANNY W. AND GOES DOWN UPON ONE KNEE.

VERENCE: Verence, King of Lancre. Do I have the honour of addressing Granny Weatherwax, doyenne of witches?

GRANNY W.: I'm she.

SHE MOTIONS AT VERENCE TO STAND UP.

VERENCE: The esteemed Nanny Ogg assisted me to leave the castle. I reasoned, if I am anchored to the stones of Lancre, then I can also go where the stones go. I am afraid I indulged in a little trickery to arrange matters. Currently I am haunting her apron.

NANNY O.: Oooohhh!

GRANNY W.: Well you'd not be the first one neither. That's for sure.

NANNY O.: Esme!

VERENCE: I beg you, Granny Weatherwax, to restore my son to the throne. It is his destiny to be King of Lancre.

GRANNY W.: Yes. Well. Destiny is tricky, you know.

VERENCE: You will not help?

GRANNY W.: It's meddling, you see. But... well, one day, when your lad is a bit older...

VERENCE: Where is he now?

GRANNY W.: We saw him safe out of the country.

NANNY O.: Very good family.

VERENCE: What kind of people? Not commoners, I trust?

GRANNY W.: Absolutely not. Not common at all. Very uncommon. In fact, er...

MAGRAT: They were Thespians.

VERENCE: Oh. Oh good.

NANNY O.: Were they? They didn't look it.

GRANNY W.: Don't show your ignorance, Gytha Ogg. Sorry about that, your majesty. She don't even know where Thespia is.

VERENCE: Well, wherever it is, I hope they know how to school a man in the arts of war. I know Felmet. In ten years he'll be dug in here like a toad in a stone. The kingdom will become shoddy and mean. Remember, good sisters, the land and the king are one.

HE FADES FROM VIEW.

NANNY O.: One what?

MAGRAT: We've got to do something! Rules or no rules!

GRANNY W.: It's very vexing.

MAGRAT: Yes; but what are you going to do?

GRANNY W.: Reflect on things. Think about it.

A RAPIDLY APPROACHING HORSE AND CART CAN BE HEARD.

MAGRAT: You don't know what to do, do you.

GRANNY W.: Nonsense. I...

MAGRAT: There's a cart coming, Granny.

MAGRAT PULLS GRANNY W. OUT OF THE CART'S WAY JUST IN TIME. THEY BOTH LAND IN A DITCH. NANNY O. DIVES INTO A BUSH.

GRANNY W. STANDS UP AND POINTS A FINGER AT THE CART.

GRANNY W.: T... t... t...

NANNY O.: It was young Neshley from over Inkcap way.

GRANNY W.: He ran us down!

MAGRAT: You could have got out of the way.

GRANNY W.: *Get out of the way?!?* We're witches! People get out of *our way!*

MAGRAT: Help me get Nanny out of this bush, will you?

GRANNY W. CLIMBS OUT OF THE DITCH AND SHAKES HER FIST AT THE BY NOW INVISIBLE CART.

GRANNY W.: That just about does it! We're witches! I'm not taking another *day* of this!

SHE POINTS A FINGER IN THE DIRECTION THE CART WAS TRAVELLING. A LONG FLARE OF LIGHT CRACKLES FROM HER FINGER.

CARTER: *(O.O.S.)* Waaaaagh!

NANNY O. IS FINALLY HELPED OUT OF HER BUSH.

GRANNY W.: Lock up a witch would he?

NANNY O.: We'd better step in here.

NANNY O. AND MAGRAT PIN GRANNY W.'S ARMS TO HER SIDES.

GRANNY W.: I'll show him what a witch could do!

NANNY O.: Yes, yes. Very good. Very *good*.

GRANNY W.: Wyrd sisters indeed!

NANNY O.: Hold her a minute, Magrat.

NANNY O. ADMINISTERS A HEFTY SLAP TO GRANNY W.

GRANNY W.: Thank you. But I meant it. We'll meet tonight at the standing stone and see what must be done.

MAGRAT: Whatever happened to the rule about not meddling?

NANNY O.: As you progress in the Craft, you'll learn there is another rule. One that Esme's obeyed all her life.

MAGRAT: What's that?

NANNY O.: When you break rules, break 'em good and hard.

10. Lancre Castle. Great Hall. Evening.

DUKE FELMET IS STARING OUT OF THE WINDOW. LADY FELMET SITS ON HER THRONE, WHILE THE FOOL STANDS NEARBY.

DUKE FELMET: Ha Ha. It works. The people mutter against the witches. If it continues like this, Fool, you shall have a knighthood.

FOOL: Ahem. Er... Marry nuncle, if'n I had a Knighthood (Night Hood), why, it would keep my ears Warm in Bedde. Ha ha ha... ha ha... ha... It's funny that, er...

LADY FELMET: It seems that words are extremely powerful.

FOOL: Indeed, lady.

LADY FELMET: Very interesting – I wonder, can your words change the past?

FOOL: More easily, I think. Because the past is what people remember and memories are but words. Who knows how a king behaved a thousand years ago? There is only recollection and stories. And plays, of course.

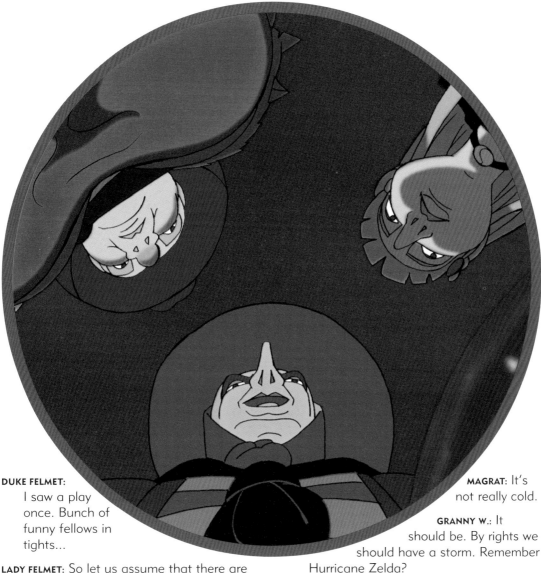

DUKE FELMET:
I saw a play once. Bunch of funny fellows in tights...

LADY FELMET: So let us assume that there are other matters, subject to controversy. Matters of historical record that have been... clouded...

DUKE FELMET: I didn't do it, you know! He slipped and fell. That was it. Slipped and fell. I wasn't even there! He attacked me. It was self-defence. That's it. He slipped and fell on his own dagger in self-defence...

LADY FELMET: Be quiet, husband. I know you didn't do it. I wasn't there with you, you may recall. It was I who didn't hand you the dagger.

11. THE MOOR. NIGHT.

THE THREE WITCHES HAVE GATHERED AT THE STANDING STONE.

GRANNY W.: Light the fire, Magrat.

MAGRAT: It's not really cold.

GRANNY W.: It should be. By rights we should have a storm. Remember Hurricane Zelda?

NANNY O.: And her amazing raining frogs? Yes. Light the fire, Magrat. There's a good girl. I dare say we'll all feel better after a nice cup of tea. With something in it.

SHE REACHES DOWN HER CLEAVAGE AND WITHDRAWS A LARGE HIP-FLASK.

MAGRAT: Alcohol is a deceiver and tarnishes the soul.

GRANNY W.: Exactly. I never touch the stuff. We should keep a clear head, Gytha.

NANNY O.: Just a drop in your tea isn't drinking. It's medicine.

NANNY O. TAKES A SWIG FROM HER HIP-FLASK.

NANNY O.: Let's curse him.

GRANNY W.: We ain't going to curse him. We're going to replace him. With his son. Proper succession.

NANNY O.: Oh, we've been through all that. In about eighteen years' time, perhaps, but...

GRANNY W.: How about tomorrow night.

NANNY O.: A child on the throne? He wouldn't last fifteen minutes.

GRANNY W.: Not a child. A grown man. Remember Black Aliss Demurrage?

NANNY O.: Esme! You ain't going to try that are you?

MAGRAT: Who was Black Aliss De...

NANNY O.: She was before your time. Before mine, really. Lived over Skund way. She was a very powerful witch.

GRANNY W.: If you listen to rumour.

NANNY O.: The biggest thing she ever did was to send a whole palace to sleep for a hundred years until... can't remember. Was there rose bushes involved? Or was it spinning wheels? I think some princess had to finger... no, there was a prince...

MAGRAT: Finger a prince?

NANNY O.: Very romantic, Black Aliss was. She liked nothing better than girl meets frog. It was on account of romance that she sent the castle to sleep.

GRANNY W.: She never sent the castle to sleep. That's just an old wives' tale. She just stirred up time a little bit. Eighteen years. That means the lad will be twenty-one at the finish. We just do the spell. He can manifest his destiny and everything will be nice and neat.

NANNY O.: Could work out nice. A bit of peace and quiet for eighteen years. If I recall the spell, after you say it, you have to fly around the castle before morning.

GRANNY W.: I wasn't thinking about that. Felmet would still be king all that time. The kingdom would still be destroyed. No. What I was thinking of doing was moving the whole kingdom.

NANNY O.: The whole of Lancre?

GRANNY W.: Yes.

NANNY O.: Eighteen years into the future?

GRANNY W.: Yes.

NANNY O. EYES GRANNY W.'S BROOMSTICK DOUBT-FULLY.

NANNY O.: You'll never do it. Not on that, not around the whole kingdom. You just couldn't carry enough magic.

GRANNY W.: I've thought of that. You're going to help.

12. LANCRE CASTLE. NIGHT.

LADY FELMET CONTINUES HER CONVERSATION WITH THE FOOL, WHILE THE DUKE STARES WITH DEPRESSION OUT OF THE WINDOW.

LADY FELMET: I was saying that perhaps there are matters that should be properly recorded.

FOOL: Marry; that you were not there at the time?

LADY FELMET: Not *where?*

FOOL: Anywhere.

LADY FELMET: But everyone has to be somewhere!

FOOL: I mean you were everywhere but at the top of the stairs.

LADY FELMET: Which stairs?

FOOL: Any stairs. I distinctly remember not seeing you!

DUKE FELMET: It was a very good play, the play that I saw. There were fights and no-one really died. Some very good speeches I thought...

LADY FELMET: Can you write a play? A play that will be remembered long after rumour has died?

FOOL: No lady. It is a special talent.

LADY FELMET: But can you find someone who has it?

FOOL: There are such people, lady.

LADY FELMET: Find one. Find the best. The truth will out.

13. STO LAT. EVENING.

IN THE TOWN OF STO LAT THE COVERED CARTS OF VITOLLER'S TRAVELLING PLAYERS ARE SEEN IN THE MARKET SQUARE.

14. COVERED CART. EVENING.

HWEL IS HARD AT WORK ON HIS LATEST PLAY.

HWEL: 'Like unto the staje of a theater ys the world, wheron alle persons strut as players...' No, no, no...

HIS THOUGHTS BECOME VISIBLE IN FRONT OF HIM. A KING BATTLES STIFFLY WITH A KNIGHT. THE KNIGHT TRANSMUTES INTO CHARLIE CHAPLIN. THE KING TURNS INTO A PORTLY MAN SPORTING A BOWLER.

HWEL: 'This is amain dainty mess you have got me into, Stanleigh...' No, that's not right either.

15. SKY OVER LANCRE. NIGHT.

MAGRAT HOVERS ON HER BROOMSTICK ABOVE LANCRE, AWAITING THE ARRIVAL OF GRANNY W.

MAGRAT: Oh dear. I hope she hasn't happened to anyone...

FROM ABOVE COMES THE SOUND OF A FAST APPROACHING BROOMSTICK.

GRANNY W.: *(O.O.S.)* Stop dreaming girl.

MAGRAT SEES GRANNY W. ABOVE HER AND FLIES UP TO MEET HER.

GRANNY W.: Not before time! I don't reckon this one's got more than a few minutes' flight left. Come on. Get a move on.

MAGRAT TOUCHES GRANNY W.'S HAND AND TRANSFERS MAGIC TO HER.

MAGRAT: Leave me a bit! I've got to get down!

GRANNY W.: Shouldn't be difficult.

MAGRAT: I mean get down safely!

SHE BEGINS TO FALL EARTHWARDS.

MAGRAT: Oooooh...

16. THE FOREST. NIGHT.

THE FOOL IS LYING BESIDE A LOG. MAGRAT FALLS THROUGH THE TREES AND LANDS ON TOP OF HIM.

MAGRAT: Hoogh!

SHE BECOMES AWARE THAT THE GROUND SHE IS SITTING ON IS MOVING. SHE LOOKS DOWN.

MAGRAT: Ohh.

FOOL: Oww!

MAGRAT: You!

FOOL: You!

MAGRAT: Did I hurt you?

FOOL: Well I've got one or two bells that won't be the same again.

17. SKY OVER LANCRE. NIGHT.

GRANNY W. URGES HER BROOMSTICK DOWN THROUGH A LARGE CLOUD.

NANNY OGG IS HOVERING WHEN SHE IS JOINED BY GRANNY W.

GRANNY W.: Well, let's have the power. I'm running out of up.

SHE REACHES OUT HER HAND AND NANNY O. TAKES IT. MAGIC FLOWS BETWEEN THEM.

GRANNY W.: Did you bring something to drink?

NANNY O.: Certainly. You said.

GRANNY W.: Well...?

NANNY O.: Well I drank it, didn't I. Sitting around here at my age.

18. THE FOREST. NIGHT.

THE FOOL AND MAGRAT ARE SITTING ON A LOG NEAR WHERE MAGRAT HAD LANDED.

MAGRAT: I wish you'd stop working for the Duke. You know what he's like. Torturing people and setting fire to their cottages and everything.

FOOL: But I'm his Fool. A Fool has to be loyal to his master. Right up until he dies. It's tradition.

MAGRAT: But you don't even like being a Fool.

FOOL: I hate it. But if I've got to be a Fool, I'll do it properly.

MAGRAT: That's really stupid.

FOOL: I prefer foolish.

19. SKY OVER LANCRE. NIGHT.

GRANNY W. IS FALLING LIKE A STONE.

GRANNY W.: Agggghh. Ice! It's iced up!

NANNY O. RUSHES DOWN ON HER BROOMSTICK AND REACHES OUT A HAND TO GRAB GRANNY W.'S SKIRT.

NANNY O.: I told you it was daft! You went through all that wet mist and then up into the cold air you daft besom!

THEY ARE STILL PLUMMETING EARTHWARDS.

GRANNY W.& NANNY O.: Aaaaaaghhh!

THEY FLY OVER THE EDGE OF LANCRE GORGE AND MANAGE TO REGAIN A LITTLE HEIGHT. GRANNY W. BANKS ROUND TO FOLLOW THE PATH OF THE RIVER.

NANNY O.: What the disc are you doing?

GRANNY W.: I can follow the river! Don't you worry!

NANNY O.: You come aboard, you hear! It's all over!

THERE IS AN EXPLOSION FROM THE REAR END OF GRANNY W.'S BROOMSTICK. AS GRANNY W. BEGINS TO FALL, NANNY O. GRABS HER UNDER THE ARMS.

NANNY O.: I can't pull you up!

GRANNY W.: Well I can't climb up, can I? Act your age, Gytha!

NANNY O. RELEASES HER HOLD ON GRANNY W. SHE FALLS EARTHWARDS, BUT IS RESCUED BY NANNY O. AND HEAVED UP TO SIT BEHIND HER ON NANNY O.'S BROOMSTICK.

GRANNY W.: Don't you ever do that again, Gytha Ogg.

NANNY O.: I promise.

GRANNY W.: Now turn us around. We're heading for Lancre Bridge.

NANNY O. HEADS OFF TOWARDS THE BRIDGE.

NANNY O.: There's still miles to go.

GRANNY W.: Don't fuss. There's still plenty of night left.

NANNY O.: Not enough, I'm thinking.

GRANNY W.: Gytha, a witch doesn't know the meaning of the word failure.

NANNY O. KNITS HER BROW AS SHE CONSIDERS THIS APPARENT NON-SEQUITUR.

NANNY O.: Esme?

GRANNY W.: What?

NANNY O.: It means 'lack of success'.

20. SKY ABOVE LANCRE BRIDGE. DAWN.

NANNY O. AND GRANNY W. FLY TOWARDS LANCRE BRIDGE.

NANNY O.: Look! Lancre Bridge!

THE BROOMSTICK FLIES DOWNWARDS AND NANNY O. LANDS BY THE BRIDGE. THE TWO WITCHES DISMOUNT.

NANNY O.: Esme, you'll go down in history for this, you know.

GRANNY W.: Do you think I will?

NANNY O.: Mark my words.

GRANNY W.: Hmm.

NANNY O.: But you've got to complete the spell, mind.

GRANNY W. RAISES HER ARMS SKYWARDS.

21. THE FOREST. NIGHT.

THE FOOL REACHES FOR MAGRAT'S HAND.

FOOL: If... if I kiss you... will I turn into a frog?

MAGRAT: We shall have to see... Hee. Hee.

THEY KISS.

1. THE FOREST. NIGHT.

THE FOOL AND MAGRAT ARE SITTING ON THE LOG, KISSING.

FOOL: Did you feel the disc move?

MAGRAT LOOKS AROUND HER.

MAGRAT: I think she's done it.

FOOL: Done what?

MAGRAT: Oh... nothing...

FOOL: It felt like we kissed through all eternity.

MAGRAT: Well, through eighteen years at least.

FOOL: Shall we have another try? I don't think we got it quite right that time.

THEY BOTH LAUGH.

2. LANCRE CASTLE. MAIN HALL. DAWN.

DUKE FELMET, EATING PORRIDGE, CASTS A MALEVOLENT GLANCE THROUGH THE WINDOW TOWARDS THE TREES.

DUKE FELMET: Trees... You trees! stop spying on me... I hate this kingdom!

3. THE FOREST. EARLY MORNING.

MAGRAT: Ankh-Morpork?!? But you'll be away for ages!

FOOL: The Duke's given me special instructions. He trusts me.

MAGRAT: But you don't have to go. You don't *want* to go.

FOOL: No, but I still have to do it. I gave my word.

MAGRAT: Just when we were getting to know each other. You're pathetic!

FOOL: I'd only be pathetic if I broke my word.

MAGRAT: Huh!

FOOL: I'm sorry. I'll be back in a few weeks. I couldn't see you again before I go, could I?

MAGRAT: I shall be washing my hair.

4. NANNY O.'S COTTAGE. MORNING.

NANNY O. AND GRANNY W. HAVE BEEN JOINED BY THE GHOST OF VERENCE.

VERENCE: Very well done. I thought it was superb. Being in the ethereal plane, of course, I was in a position to observe closely.

GRANNY W.: Anyway. We've got to find the boy now. That's the next step. He'll be in Ankh-Morpork; mark my words. Everyone ends up there.

5. ANKH-MORPORK. NIGHT.

VITOLLER AND TOMJON ARE STANDING ON THE STAGE OF A NEWLY CONSTRUCTED, UNFINISHED BUILDING.

VITOLLER: I said I'd do it, laddie, and I have. All those years ago, when first you trod the boards... But... I don't know. Maybe it's against nature, capturing the spirit of the theatre and putting it in a cage. And I'm going to find it hard settling down at my time of life.

TOMJON: It's not doing you any good. You're not getting any younger. You'll do better to stay put here and let people come to us. And they will, too. You know the crowds we're getting now. Hwel's plays are famous.

VITOLLER: Damn thing hasn't even got a name. I should call it 'The Gold Mine'. That's what it's costing me!

TOMJON: It needs a name that means everything. Because there's everything inside it. The whole world on the stage, do you see? How about, The Dysk!

6. HWEL'S ROOM. NIGHT.

HWEL SITS WRITING AT HIS DESK.

HWEL: In a Hand Bag !

TOMJON: 'Night, Hwel.

AS HWEL WRITES, THE IMAGES OF THE MARX BROTHERS APPEAR ABOVE HIS HEAD.

HWEL: First Clown: *(GROUCHO MARX VOICE)*
'This iss My Little Study. Hey, with a Little Study, youe could goe a long way. And I wish youed start now. Iffe you can't leave in a cab then leave yn a huff. Iff that's too soon, thenn leave in a minute and a huff.' Second Clown: *(CHICO MARX VOICE)* 'Atsa right, Boss.' Third Clown – business with bladder on a stick – honk honk... Hoogh. Yes, it's funny. But is it right?

HWEL BEGINS TO WRITE AGAIN.

HWEL: *(READS)* 'All the Disc is but an theater. And alle men and wymmen are but players...'

7. TOMJON'S ROOM. NIGHT.

TOMJON LIES SLEEPING ON HIS BED.

HWEL: *(O.O.S.)* '...except those who sell popcorn.'

TOMJON'S DREAM BECOMES APPARENT. THE WALL BULGES OUT AND THREE DISTORTED FACES COME AND GO AS THEY LOOK AT HIM.

WITCHES: All hail...

NANNY O.: Erm... Verence?

GRANNY W.: No. That was the *old* king.

NANNY O.: And jinglebells.

MAGRAT: Who?

NANNY O.: Your young feller. Him with the bells and the eyes like a septic bloodhound.

GRANNY W.: We'll just keep on calling him Tomjon.

NANNY O.: Oh, have it your way, Esme.

GRANNY W.: I will, thank you very much. All hail Tomjon...

NANNY O.: Who shall be king hereafter!

MAGRAT: Here after what?

GRANNY W.: Just hereafter, girl.

NANNY O.: It's what you're supposed to say.

GRANNY W.: You might try and make an effort. He can't hear us, can he? He's tossing and turning a bit.

NANNY O.: You know I've never been able to get sound on this thing, Esme.

GRANNY W.: Huh. Should've got yourself a proper one.

NANNY O.: What about you? You haven't got one at all!

MAGRAT: Please, don't let's start...

TOMJON SITS UP IN BED.

TOMJON: Aagh!

HWEL: What's up lad? Nightmares?

TOMJON: Gods. It was terrible. It was like... I was sort of inside something, like a bowl, and there were these three faces peering in at me.

HWEL: Funny old things, dreams.

TOMJON: Not much funny about that one.

TOMJON STANDS UP.

TOMJON: What's the time?

HWEL: It's after midnight. And you know what your father said about going to bed late.

TOMJON STANDS UP.

TOMJON: I'm not. I'm getting up early. Getting up early is very healthy. I'm going out for a drink. You can come too; to keep an eye on me.

HWEL: You also know what your father says about going out drinking.

TOMJON: Yes. He said he used to do it all the time when he was a lad. He said he'd think nothing of quaffing ale all night and coming home at 5 a.m.

HWEL: All right. Just the one though. Somewhere decent.

TOMJON: I promise. By the way; exactly how does one quaff?

THEY EXIT.

8. THE MENDED DRUM. NIGHT.

HWEL AND TOMJON WALK DOWN THE STREET TOWARDS THE TAVERN.

TOMJON: I reckon they're roistering in here, don't you?

A MAN FLIES BACKWARDS THROUGH THE AIR OUT OF THE PUB AND LANDS IN A PUDDLE ON THE OTHER SIDE OF THE STREET.

HWEL: It looks like it.

9. THE MENDED DRUM. NIGHT.

TOMJON AND HWEL SURVEY THE MENDED DRUM AND ITS CLIENTELE.

TOMJON: What a swamp!

HWEL: In a swamp, the alligators don't pick your pockets first.

THEY ARRIVE AT THE BAR, BEHIND WHICH HIBISCUS DUNELM IS SERVING.

TOMJON: Two pints of your finest ale, landlord!

THE CROWD FALLS SILENT. HWEL FINDS THAT HE IS BEING STARED AT BY A RED-BEARDED AXE-MAN.

REDBEARD: What we got here? A flipping lawn ornament? Where's your fishing rod?

HIBISCUS: Here you are. One pint. And one half pint.

REDBEARD EMPTIES HIS TANKARD OVER HWEL.

REDBEARD: I'm not drinking here again. It's bad enough they let monkeys drink in here...

HE INDICATES THE LIBRARIAN SITTING IN THE CORNER.

LIBRARIAN: Oooook.

HE GLOWERS AT REDBEARD.

HIBISCUS: Er... I don't think you meant that, did you? Not about monkeys, eh? You didn't really, did you?

REDBEARD: A monkey's a monkey. But lawn ornaments...

AFTER A SCUFFLE, THE LIBRARIAN GRABS REDBEARD'S AXE AND EMBEDS IT IN THE COUNTER.

LIBRARIAN: Ooooooks.

HIBISCUS: Holymurrogods!

THE LIBRARIAN PUNCHES REDBEARD AND A GENERAL FIGHT BREAKS OUT.

TOMJON: Is this real roistering, do you suppose, or merely rollicking?

HWEL: It's going to be full-blooded murder in a minute, my lad!

MAGRAT: (V.O.) He will make friends easy.

TOMJON: Brothers! Please! Pray silence!

SILENCE FALLS.

TOMJON: Brothers! Yea, brothers! I may call all men brother and clasp them hardly to my heart. Oh, who against his brother would his hand in anger raise? Not I. Nor you! For anger is the ebon worm whose fell and poison jaws devour us all; yes even to the very soul. Cast out this demon anger and in his stead play host to amity, to friendship...and to love!

HIS WORDS MOVE HIS AUDIENCE TO TEARS.

HWEL: Come away now, before it wears off.

HE LEADS TOMJON TOWARDS THE DOOR.

10. THE MENDED DRUM. NIGHT.

TOMJON AND HWEL LEAVE THE PUB.

TOMJON: Right. Where shall we go next?

HWEL: *Next?!?*

THE FIGHT BREAKS OUT AGAIN INSIDE THE MENDED DRUM AS THEY WALK OFF.

11. STREET IN ANKH-MORPORK. NIGHT.

TOMJON AND HWEL APPEAR NEAR THE CAVERN.

TOMJON: Ah! A troll tavern. I'd like to see a troll tavern.

HWEL: They're for trolls only, boy. Molten lava to drink and rock music and cheese and chutney flavoured pebbles.

TOMJON: Perhaps you're right.

THEY WALK OFF.

12. THE DYSK THEATRE. NIGHT.

CHRYSOPHASE AND VITOLLER ARE STANDING ON THE STAGE.

VITOLLER: But my good man... If I could explain.

CHRYSOPHASE: Listen up, Littler...

VITOLLER: Vitoller.

CHRYSOPHASE: Whatever. I ain't no man, and I sure as Shades ain't good. I lent you the money in good faith. And now I want it back.

VITOLLER: You'll... you'll have to give me time!

CHRYSOPHASE: I'll give you time.

VITOLLER: Thank you! I...

CHRYSOPHASE: Till tomorrow.

VITOLLER: To... tomorrow?!? But...

CHRYSOPHASE: I ain't running no charity. Tomorrow. Heh heh heh.

CHRYSOPHASE LEAVES; VITOLLER WATCHES HIM GLOOMILY.

13. A STREET IN ANKH-MORPORK. NIGHT.

TOMJON CONTINUES HIS QUEST FOR THE NEXT WATERING HOLE. HWEL FOLLOWS RELUCTANTLY.

TOMJON: What about a dwarf bar?

HWEL: You'd hate it. Besides, you'd run out of headroom.

TOMJON: Low dives, are they?

HWEL: Look at it like this. How long do you think you could sing about gold?

TOMJON: It's yellow, and chinks and you buy things with it... About four seconds I think.

HWEL: Right. Gets a bit repetitive after five hours.

THE SOUND OF A SCUFFLE IS HEARD FROM A DARK ALLEY.

FOOL: Gwwwlllmmmnnnff... ouch!

TOMJON: Did you hear something?

TOMJON RUNS DOWN THE ALLEY TO INVESTIGATE. HWEL FOLLOWS.

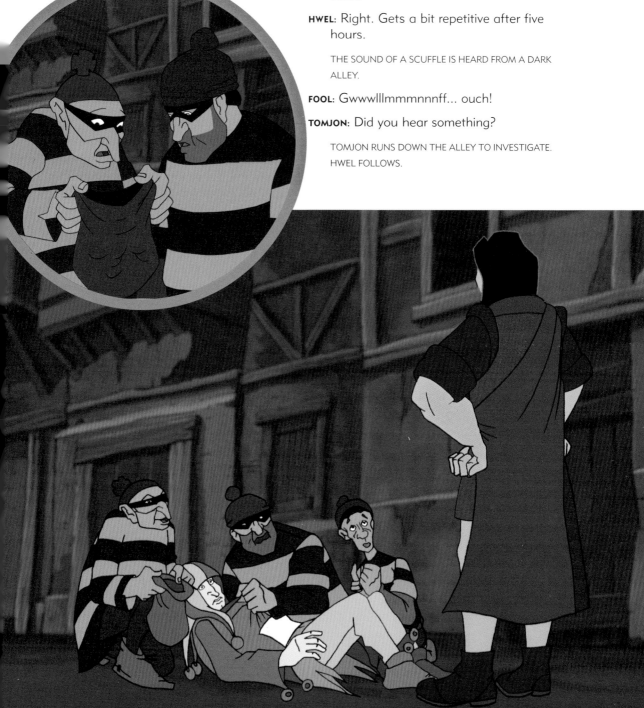

14. DARK ALLEY. NIGHT.

THREE THIEVES ARE STRUGGLING WITH THE FOOL. TOMJON RUNS UP.

TOMJON: Oi!

HWEL: They're mugging a clown.

TOMJON: What's going on here?

BOGGIS HANDS TOMJON HIS CARD.

TOMJON: 'J.H. Flannelfoot Boggis and nephews, bespoke thieves. Let us quote you for our family rate.' They're from the Thieves' Guild.

BOGGIS: That's right. Only don't expect us to do you, cos we're on our way home.

TOMJON: But you were kicking him!

FOOL: Ooorgh!

ASSISTANT 1: Worl, not a lot. Not what you'd call actual kicking.

ASSISTANT 2: More foot nudging, sort of thing.

TOMJON: How much did you steal?

BOGGIS PEERS INSIDE THE PURSE.

BOGGIS: Oh swipe me! There must be a hundred silver dollars in here! I can't handle that sort of money! You've got to be in the League of Lawyers to steal that much!

TOMJON: Give it back to him, then.

BOGGIS: But I done him a receipt!

THE FOOL GROANS.

TOMJON: Look after him. I'll sort this out.

HE GOES BACK TO THE THIEVES.

TOMJON: My client feels that the situation could be resolved if you give the money back.

BOGGIS: Ye-es... but it's the receipt, see. We have to fill it up. Time and place, signed and everything.

TOMJON: My client feels that possibly you could rob him of, let us say, five copper pieces...

FOOL: *(O.O.S.)* No I don't!

TOMJON: ...that represents two copper pieces as the going rate, plus expenses of three copper pieces for time, call-out fees...

BOGGIS: Wear and tear on the cosh...

TOMJON: Exactly.

BOGGIS: Very fair. Very fair.

BOGGIS TAKES A DOLLAR FROM THE PURSE, PUTS IN SOME CHANGE AND HANDS THE PURSE TO TOMJON.

BOGGIS: And er... How about something for the weekend sir? We've got a special on G.B.H. this season. Practically painless.

ASSISTANT 1: Hardly breaks the skin.

ASSISTANT 2: Plus you get a choice of limb.

TOMJON: Thank you. No.

BOGGIS: Oh. Well. Right you are then. No problem.

THE THIEVES BEGIN TO WALK AWAY.

TOMJON: Which merely leaves the question of my legal fees...

THE THIEVES STOP DEAD IN THEIR TRACKS.

15. STREET IN ANKH-MORPORK. NIGHT.

TOMJON, HWEL AND THE FOOL ARE APPROACHING A DWARVISH TAVERN. TOMJON PASSES THE FOOL HIS PURSE.

TOMJON: Three silver dollars and eighteen copper pieces in profit.

FOOL: That was amazing! I mean the way they volunteered to go home and get some more money as well. And the youngest one started to cry. Amazing. Well, I'm very grateful. I'd really like to show my gratitude.

HE STOPS OUTSIDE THE TAVERN.

FOOL: Tell you what, let me treat you to a drink. It's the least I can do. After you.

HE OPENS THE DOOR AND GESTURES FOR TOMJON TO ENTER FIRST. TOMJON, ON THE OTHER SIDE OF THE DOOR, MAKES THE SAME GESTURE.

TOMJON: No after you.

FOR THE FIRST TIME A SIMILARITY BETWEEN THE FOOL AND TOMJON IS NOTICEABLE AS THEY STAND

ONE ON EACH SIDE OF THE TAVERN DOOR. TOMJON ENTERS.

HWEL RUBS HIS EYES AND SHAKES HIS HEAD IN DISBELIEF.

HWEL: No. Trick of the light.

THE FOOL ENTERS THE TAVERN, FOLLOWED BY HWEL.

16. DWARVISH TAVERN. NIGHT.

HWEL, TOMJON AND THE FOOL SIT AT A TABLE.

FOOL: I reckon... I reckon I could do with another drink! My shout this time! Hahahaha. My squeak! Hahahahaaaarghh! Ow!

HE STANDS UP AND BANGS HIS HEAD ON THE CEILING. HWEL ADDRESSES HIS SILENT FELLOW DWARVES.

HWEL: S'all right. He don't mean it. Don't know many dwarfs.

FOOL: Yeh. Bit *short* of them where I come from. Hahahaha.

A DWARF, GRABPOT THUNDERGUST, APPROACHES HIM, TOSSING AN AXE UP AND DOWN.

GRABPOT: I think you ought to try and be a bit less funny. Otherwise you'll be amusing the demons in the dungeon dimension.

HWEL: Here, I know you. You got a cosmetics mill down Hobfast Street. I bought a load of greasepaint off you last week...

GRABPOT: Shhh. Shuttup.

TOMJON: Ver' good stuff. Specially your No. 19 Corpse Green. My father swears by it.

GRABPOT: Here, you're not with the theatre?

TOMJON: Tha's us. Strolling Players. Standing still players, now. Ha ha. Sliding down players...

GRABPOT: I went last week. Och, it was that guid. There was this girl and this fellow, but he was married. And there was this other fellow and they said he'd died, and she pined away and took poison, but then it turned out this man was the other man really. Everyone died in the end. Very tragic. I cried all the way home.

THE FOOL LOOKS FROM HWEL TO TOMJON AND BACK AGAIN.

FOOL: Here, you two with the theatre?

TOMJON: S'right.

FOOL: Then I've come five hundred miles to find you.

HE TAKES HIS BAG OF MONEY AND PLONKS IT ON THE TABLE IN FRONT OF HIM.

17. LANCRE CASTLE. FELMET BEDROOM. NIGHT.

FELMET IS WRINGING HIS HANDS AND PACING.

FELMET: It was a very good play that I saw – Let him come when he is grown.
Ha. Ha. Ha!

HE SHOUTS OUT OF THE WINDOW.

FELMET: I HATE this kingdom!

LADY FELMET: Be quiet, husband.

18. THE DYSK THEATRE. EARLY MORNING.

THE ROOM IS STILL BEING DECORATED.

TOMJON AND VITOLLER ARE IN CONFERENCE; HWEL SITS AT HIS DESK, NURSING A HANGOVER. THE FOOL SITS TO ONE SIDE OF THE ROOM, SIMILARLY HUNG-OVER. HIS PURSE, BULGING WITH SILVER, IS ON THE DESK IN FRONT OF HWEL. VITOLLER TRIES TO ENGAGE THE FOOL IN CONVERSATION, BUT HIS EYES KEEP WANDERING TO THE BAG OF MONEY.

VITOLLER: Where did you say he'd come from?

HWEL: The Ramtops. Some little kingdom no-one has ever heard of.

FOOL: Lancre.

HWEL: Sounds like a chest infection.

TOMJON: That's where I was born. When you did a tour of the mountains.

THERE IS A PREGNANT PAUSE WHILE VITOLLER TRIES ONCE AGAIN TO AVOID THE PULL OF THE MONEY.

VITOLLER: Tomjon. Laddie. It's a long, long way...

TOMJON: I could take some of the younger lads. We could be back by Soulcake Day in time for a Grand Opening...

HWEL: I've got to write the damn thing first.

THE FOOL LOOKS UP AND POINTS TO THE MONEY.

FOOL: There's more where that came from if you do. Another hundred silver pieces, her ladyship said.

TOMJON: It sounds interesting. Wicked king ruling with the help of evil witches. Storms. Ghastly forests. True heir to the throne in life-or-death struggle. Flash of dagger. Screams. Alarums. Evil king dies, good triumphs, bells ring out.

FOOL: Groogh!

VITOLLER: But... my dear boy... are you sure you really want to do it? On the other hand, what harm could it do? The pay's the... the play's the thing! And I do have some debts...

CHRYSOPHASE APPEARS IN THE DOORWAY.

HWEL: Chrysophase!

TOMJON: He's the one that has people's limbs torn off!

HWEL: How much do you owe him?

CHRYSOPHASE: An arm and a leg. So. You've got the money.

HE EYES THE BAG.

TOMJON: How much does he owe you?

CHRYSOPHASE: Let's see now. A hundred silver pieces?

VITOLLER: A hundred? I only borrowed...

CHRYSOPHASE SNATCHES THE BAG OF MONEY AND PUTS IT IN HIS POCKET.

CHRYSOPHASE: And then there's the interest... Shall we say another hundred? After all, you wouldn't want anything to happen to your theatre. Not to mention...

HE TAKES VITOLLER'S ARM AND EYES IT WITH INTEREST.

CHRYSOPHASE: I'm not a vindictive troll. I'll give you two months. Should be enough time to get there and back.

CHRYSOPHASE LEAVES, THE MONEY JINGLING IN HIS POCKET.

CHRYSOPHASE: Heh heh heh.

TOMJON TURNS TO VITOLLER.

TOMJON: How could you have been so... stupid.

VITOLLER: I did it for you two! You deserves a better stage; a proper job. It's no life out on the road giving two performances to a bunch of farmers who throw potatoes at the stage! I said blow the cost! I just wanted you to...

HWEL: All right! Looks like I'll have to write it.

TOMJON: And I'll act it!

VITOLLER: Thank you, both.

19. ROCKY PLAIN. DAY.

THE CARTS CONTINUE THEIR JOURNEY TOWARDS LANCRE. THE THREE WITCHES ARE WATCHING THE PROGRESS OF THE PLAYERS IN NANNY OGG'S CRYSTAL BALL. NANNY O. AND GRANNY W. SIT AT THE TABLE IN MAGRAT'S COTTAGE. MAGRAT STANDS BEHIND THEM.

NANNY O.: He's definitely on his way. In a cart. A fiery white charger would have been favourite.

MAGRAT: Has he got a magic sword? We could make him one out of thunderbolt iron. I've got a spell for that. You take some thunderbolt iron... and... and then... you make a sword out of it.

GRANNY W.: You're a disgrace, the pair of you. Magic chargers... fiery swords. I can't be having with that old stuff.

NANNY O.: It's a long road. There's many a slip twixt dress and drawers. There could be bandits.

GRANNY W.: We shall watch over him.

MAGRAT: That's not right. He ought to be able to fight his own battles.

NANNY O.: We don't want him to go wasting his strength. We want him good and fresh for when he gets here.

MAGRAT: And then we'll leave him to fight his battles in his own way?

GRANNY W.: Provided he looks like winning.

20. ROCKY PLAIN. DAY.

IN THE FIRST CART, HWEL SITS NEXT TO TOMJON, WHO HOLDS THE REINS. HWEL IS MAKING A FEW ADJUSTMENTS TO HIS SCRIPT. HE READS.

HWEL: '1st Witch: He's late. *(PAUSE)*'
'2nd Witch: He said he would come. *(PAUSE)*'
'3rd Witch: This is my last newt. I saved it for him. And he hasn't come. *(PAUSE)*'

TOMJON: I think you ought to slow it down a bit. No-one said it had to sparkle.

HWEL: It could you know. If I could just get it right.

TOMJON: I think we're lost.

A GANG OF BANDITS APPEARS BRANDISHING RUSTY OLD SWORDS. THE CHIEF BANDIT LEERS AT THEM.

CHIEF: Well now. What have we here?

HWEL: We've got a receipt somewhere...

TOMJON: They don't look like Guild Thieves. They look like freelancers to me. Could I just say something?

CHIEF: You're going to beg for mercy, right?

TOMJON: That's right. The point I'd like to make is that... The worth of man lies not in feats of arms. Or the fiery hunger of the ravening horde.

THE WITCHES ARE WATCHING PROCEEDINGS IN THE CRYSTAL BALL.

GRANNY W.: Pass me that milk jug, Magrat.

MAGRAT DOES SO.

MAGRAT: That was a present from my aunt.

21. ROCKY PLAIN. DAY.

TOMJON IS FINISHING HIS SPEECH. ALL THE BANDITS ARE WON OVER, EXCEPT THE CHIEF.

TOMJON: Become a man! This jewel of jewels, this crown of crowns.

CHIEF: Is that it?

TOMJON: Well... yes.

CHIEF: It was a good speech. But I don't see what it's got to do with me. Hand over your valuables.

HE HOLDS A SWORD TO TOMJON'S THROAT. THE MILK JUG, WITH ITS PAY-LOAD OF FROZEN MILK, LANDS ON THE CHIEF'S HEAD. HE FALLS BACK, POLE-AXED.

TOMJON: I don't think he was very impressed with my performance.

HWEL: A born critic.

THE FOUR CARTS RECOMMENCE THEIR JOURNEY.

22. Magrat's Cottage. Day.

MAGRAT: You can't get jugs like that any more. I mean, if you said what was on your mind, there was a flat-iron on the shelf. A week ago she said she wouldn't interfere.

NANNY O.: A week's a long time in thaumaturgics. Eighteen years for one thing.

GRANNY W.'S ATTENTION IS STILL FIRMLY FIXED ON THE CRYSTAL BALL.

GRANNY W.: They're wandering all over the place. They may be good at the theatre but they've got something to learn about travelling.

23. Mountain Foothills. Day.

HWEL IS WORKING ON HIS PLAY AGAIN. TOMJON IS LOOKING AT THE SURROUNDING COUNTRYSIDE.

TOMJON: You've got us lost, haven't you.

HWEL: Certainly not.

TOMJON: Well, where are we, then?

HWEL: The mountains. Perfectly clear on any atlas.

TOMJON: We ought to stop and ask someone.

HWEL: Who did you have in mind?

TOMJON POINTS OVER TO A CLUMP OF BUSHES. A TALL, BLACK HAT CAN BE SEEN BEHIND IT, BOBBING UP AND DOWN.

TOMJON: That old woman in the funny hat. I've been watching her. She keeps ducking down behind a bush when she thinks I'm looking.

HWEL TURNS AND SEES THE HAT.

HWEL: Ho there, good mother!

GRANNY W. POPS UP BEHIND THE BUSH.

GRANNY W.: Who're you calling mother?

HWEL: Just a figure of speech Mrs... miss...

GRANNY W.: Mistress. And I'm a poor old woman gathering wood. Lawks. Ahem. You did give me a fright, young master. My poor old heart.

TOMJON: I'm sorry?

GRANNY W.: What?

TOMJON: Your poor old heart what?

GRANNY W.: What about my poor old heart?

HWEL: It's just that you mentioned it.

GRANNY W.: Well, it isn't important. Lawks. I expect you're looking for Lancre.

TOMJON: Well, yes.

GRANNY W.: You've come too far. Go back about two miles, and take the track on the right, past the stand of pines.

WILMSLOE, AN APPRENTICE PLAYER, STICKS HIS HEAD OUT FROM BEHIND HWEL AND TOMJON.

WILMSLOE: Psst – When you meet a mysterious old lady in the road, you've got to offer to share your lunch with her.

TOMJON: You have?

WILMSLOE: It's terribly bad luck not to.

TOMJON: Would you care to share our lunch, good moth... old wom... ma'am?

GRANNY W.: What is it?

TOMJON: Salt pork.

GRANNY W. SNIFFS AND TURNS ON HER HEEL.

GRANNY W.: Gives me wind.

SHE STALKS OFF. TOMJON GEES UP THE HORSE AND TURNS THE CART AROUND. THE OTHERS FOLLOW.

24. MOUNTAIN FOOTHILLS. DAY.

THE CARTS CONTINUE.

TOMJON: She could have given more explicit instructions.

TOMJON HAS SEEN SOMEONE AMONG THE PINE TREES.

HWEL: What? Like ask at the next crone? Look over there.

IT IS MAGRAT.

TOMJON: Ho there, old... good...

MAGRAT: Wood-gatherer.

TOMJON: Would you care to share our lunch, old... good wo... miss. It's only salt pork, I'm afraid.

MAGRAT: Meat is extremely bad for the digestive system. If you could see the inside of your colon, you'd be horrified. *(PAUSES)* Er... I am just a humble... oh. I mean, *lawks*, I'm just a humble wood-gatherer, lawks, collecting a few sticks and mayhap directing lost travellers on the road to Lancre. Lawks.

HWEL: I thought we'd get to that.

MAGRAT: You fork left up ahead and turn right at the big stone with the crack in it. You can't miss it. Lawks – Lawks!

THE CARTS CONTINUE ON THEIR WAY.

25. MOUNTAIN FOOTHILLS. DAY.

THE CARTS ARE AT A STANDSTILL. HWEL SITS WITH ARMS CROSSED. TOMJON IS PUZZLED.

TOMJON: What are we doing?

HWEL: Waiting.

TOMJON: It'll be getting dark soon.

HWEL: We won't be here long.

NANNY OGG, DRESSED AS A WOOD-GATHERER, APPROACHES THEM.

HWEL: It's salt pork. Take it or leave it. Now. Which way's Lancre?

NANNY O.: Keep on left at the ravine, then you pick up the track that leads to a bridge. You can't miss it.

HWEL: You forgot about the lawks.

NANNY O.: Oh yeah. Sorry. Lawks.

HWEL: And you're a humble old wood-gatherer, I expect.

NANNY O.: Dead right.

SHE BEGINS TO CLIMB UP INTO THE CART.

NANNY O.: And I wouldn't say no to a lift. Move over.

NANNY O. SETTLES DOWN NEXT TO HWEL.

NANNY O.: You mentioned salt pork. There wouldn't be any mustard would there?

HWEL: No.

NANNY O.: Can't abide salt pork without condiments. But pass it over anyway. What's in that leather bottle?

TOMJON: Beer.
HWEL: Water. _(TOGETHER)_

NANNY O. TAKES A SWIG.

NANNY O.: _(O.O.S.)_ Pretty weak stuff. Has any-one got a light?

WILMSLOE: _(O.O.S.)_ Here.

NANNY O.: _(O.O.S.)_ Good boy. Now. Has anyone got any baccy?

26. LANCRE CASTLE. EVENING.

THE CARTS TRUNDLE UP THE PATH TOWARDS THE CASTLE.

DUKE FELMET: _(V.O.)_ Ha. Ha. Ha.

27. LANCRE CASTLE. NIGHT.

DUKE FELMET SITS ON HIS THRONE IN THE GREAT HALL, HOLDING HWEL'S SCRIPT. HIS WIFE SITS BESIDE HIM. THE FOOL STANDS BEFORE THE PAIR.

DUKE FELMET: Perfect.

FOOL: Thank you.

DUKE FELMET: They've got it absolutely spot on. They might almost have been there. Ha ha.

THE DUKE CONTINUES TO LEAF THROUGH THE PAGES OF THE PLAY.

DUKE FELMET: Exactly right. This is exactly, exactly, exactly how it was.

LADY FELMET: Will have been.

DUKE FELMET: You're in this too. Amazing. It's word for word how it will be remembered.

HE LOOKS UP FROM THE MANUSCRIPT AND STARES AT THE FOOL.

DUKE FELMET: I see it's got Death in it.

FOOL: Always popular. People expect Him.

DUKE FELMET: How soon will they be here?

28. LANCRE CASTLE. EVENING.

THE TRAVELLING PLAYERS' CARTS ARE TRUNDLING OVER THE BRIDGE AND THROUGH THE GATES INTO LANCRE CASTLE. THE DUKE'S LAUGHTER ECHOES ACROSS THE KINGDOM.

DUKE FELMET: ...hahahahahahaha...

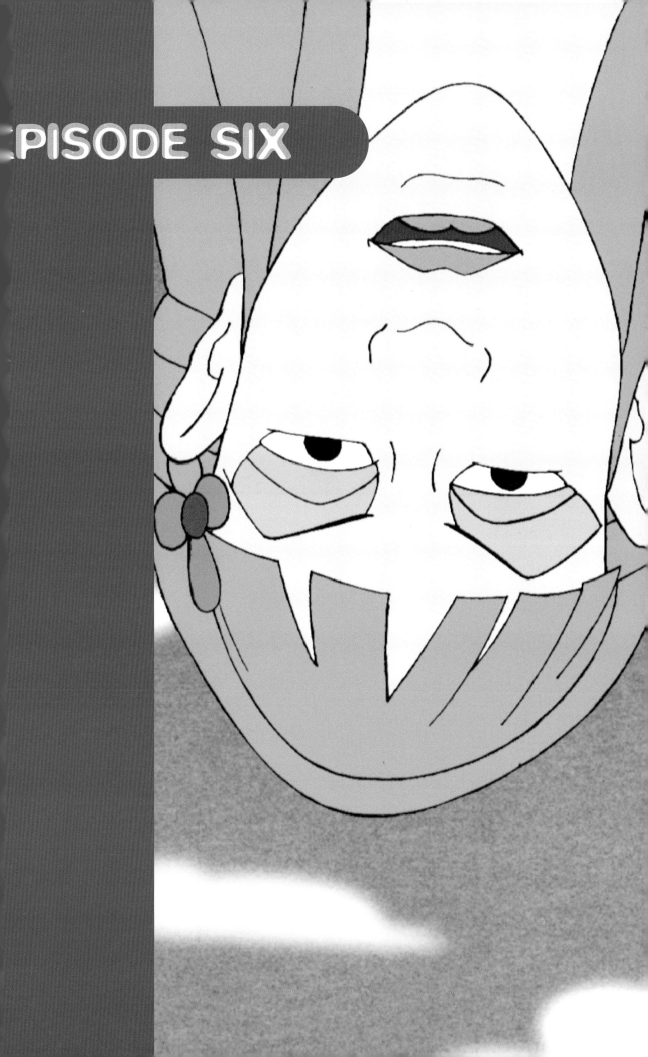

1. MEADOW. DAY

THE FOOL IS LYING ON HIS BACK BY THE POND.

A FEW SMALL CLOUDS DRIFT ACROSS THE BLUE SKY. MAGRAT'S FACE SUDDENLY APPEARS, BLOTTING OUT THE CLOUDS. SHE DOESN'T LOOK HAPPY.

MAGRAT: What's all this about a play?

MAGRAT STANDS OVER THE FOOL, WHO HAS SAT UP HURRIEDLY.

FOOL: Oh, my lord wants something to convince the people that he is the rightful king of Lancre.

MAGRAT: It's disgusting.

FOOL: I suppose you prefer the duchess's approach? She just thinks they ought to kill everyone.

MAGRAT: When's this play going to be, then?

FOOL: I'm not allowed to tell you. The duke said to me, he said, don't tell the witches.

MAGRAT: I shouldn't then.

FOOL: He said not to say that it's at eight o'clock. But meet for sherry beforehand at seven thirty, i'faith. The duke will be expecting you. Can I see you after the show?

MAGRAT IS STILL A LITTLE MIFFED WITH THE FOOL.

MAGRAT: I think I might be washing my hair again.

SHE GETS TO HER FEET. THE FOOL REACHES INSIDE HIS DOUBLET.

FOOL: I brought you this present.

MAGRAT IS ALREADY ON HER WAY AS THE FOOL PRODUCES A NECKLACE. IT DANGLES FORLORNLY FROM HIS FINGERS.

2. LANCRE CASTLE. EVENING.

THE THREE WITCHES APPEAR.

GRANNY W.: If he wants us to be there, I don't want to go. He's got some plan. He's using headology on us.

MAGRAT: There's something up. He had his men set fire to three cottages in our village last night. He always does that when he's in a good mood.

NANNY O.: Come on. All the sherry will be gone.

3. LANCRE CASTLE. EVENING.

THE FOOL IS WAITING BY THE WICKET GATE AT THE BACK OF THE CASTLE. THE WITCHES ARRIVE, GRANNY W. AND MAGRAT LOOKING GRIM.

NANNY O.: Wotcha Jinglebells!

FOOL: Oh! There's not going to be any trouble, is there? Please?

GRANNY W. BARGES PAST HIM.

GRANNY W.: I'm sure I don't know what you mean.

NANNY O.: I hope you haven't been keeping our girl here up late o' nights!

MAGRAT: Nanny!

NANNY O. FOLLOWS GRANNY W. INTO THE CASTLE COURTYARD. MAGRAT, MAKING TO FOLLOW NANNY O., IS TAKEN GENTLY BY THE ELBOW.

FOOL: I know where we can get a lovely view from one of the gate towers. And there's a cistern of water and a fireplace that the guards use sometimes.

MAGRAT FOLLOWS THE OTHER WITCHES.

FOOL: In case you want to wash your hair.

DEATH AND BINKY LAND ON THE BATTLEMENTS. DEATH LOOKS AROUND AND THEN DOWN INTO THE COURTYARD BELOW, WHERE THE AUDIENCE ARE BEGINNING TO TAKE THEIR PLACES FOR THE START OF THE PLAY.

DEATH MAKES HIS WAY ALONG THE BATTLEMENTS UNTIL HE COMES TO A DOOR IN THE WALL. HE ENTERS.

NANNY O. AND GRANNY W. ARE SEATED IN THE AUDIENCE. THEY LEAVE THE THIRD SEAT EMPTY NEXT TO NANNY O. ON THE OTHER SIDE OF THE EMPTY SEAT, AND UNNOTICED BY THE TWO WITCHES, SITS DEATH. NANNY O. PRODUCES A BAG OF NUTS.

NANNY O. OFFERS HER BAG OF WALNUTS TO THE SEEMINGLY UNOCCUPIED SEAT.

NANNY O.: Walnut?

VERENCE: No thank you. They go right through me, you know.

VERENCE TURNS TO DEATH.

VERENCE: Oh hello! Here on business?

DUKE AND LADY FELMET ARRIVE TO A FANFARE OF TRUMPETS.

DUKE FELMET: People of Lancre! You are here tonight to pay witness to a remarkable performance, one that I hope will lay many ghosts to rest. The things that you are about to see actually happened. The rest, as they say, is history. Thank you.

AS AN ACTOR STEPS IN FRONT OF THE CURTAIN TO SPEAK THE PROLOGUE, A HUSH DESCENDS UPON THE AUDIENCE.

PROLOGUE: Pray, gentles all, list to our tale,

An historie both dark and true.

Will evil triumph or will good prevail?

And what a mixture will the witches brew?

These questions all will swiftly
    answered be

By our troupe of actors as you will
    shortly see.

GRANNY W.: What's a gentle?

NANNY O.: (MOUTH FULL) Type of maggot.

SHE SPITS HER WALNUT OUT.

NANNY O.: These walnuts are damn tough. I'm going to have to take my shoe off to this one.

GRANNY W.: Actors! As if the world weren't full of enough history without inventing more. I want the world the way it is. The way it was. The past used to be a lot better than it is now.

4. BACKSTAGE. EVENING.

BEHIND THE SCENES, HWEL IS WATCHING THE PLAY, FOLLOWING THE LINES IN THE MANUSCRIPT.

OLD MAN: (O.O.S.) What hath befell the land?

OLD WOMAN: (O.O.S.) 'tis a terror by the name of king,

Who burns our houses, puts our kindred
    to the sword.

His soldiers, quick his business to
    attend,

Last night our daughter ravish'd, and
    three sheep!

But soft. No more may I say now.

BEHIND HWEL, VARIOUS APPRENTICE PLAYERS ARE STRUGGLING WITH COSTUMES AND PROPS. A COUPLE ARE TRYING TO BECOME SOLDIERS OF THE KING.

HWEL: C'mon! Soldiers of the king at the double!

HE RUNS OVER TO THEM, BUSTLING THEM TOWARDS THE STAGE.

HWEL: And the witches – where are the blasted witches?!?

THREE MORE APPRENTICE PLAYERS APPEAR.

WITCH 1: I've lost my wart.

WITCH 2: The cauldron's all full of yuk.

WITCH 3: There's something living in this wig.

HWEL: Calm down! Calm down! It'll be all right on the night!

SOLDIER 1: (O.O.S.) Ho there old crone!

SOLDIER 2: (O.O.S.) We come with orders from the king.

SOLDIER 1: (O.O.S.) Your house and all that it contains are forfeit.

OLD WOMAN: (O.O.S.) No! No! This cannot be! Hold your tongues or by my faith I'll now... I'll now... erm...

HWEL: Avenge the terror of my daughter's death!

OLD WOMAN: (O.O.S.) Avenge the terror of my daughter's death!

SOLDIER 1: (O.O.S.) Bold words indeed for one so long in years. What say'st thou, Dickon?

SOLDIER 2: (O.O.S.) Mayhap a lesson this old crone could learn. And learn it from the blade of this, my sword!

OLD WOMAN: (O.O.S.) Strike now! I care no more for this cruel world the king here hath us brought. My death a blest relief will be; for I shall at last with my dear husband lie.

HWEL TURNS TO THE WITCHES.

HWEL: Right. Now what are you? You're scheming evil secret black and midnight hags! Tell me what you are!

WITCHES: We're scheming evil secret...

TOMJON ARRIVES, DRESSED AS A KING.

TOMJON: Hwel? There's no crown! I've got to wear a crown!

HWEL: Of course there's a crown! The big one with the red glass. We used it in that place with the big square...

TOMJON: I think we left it there.

HWEL: Well, just find another one then! In the props box. You're the Evil King, you've got to have a crown! Get on with it lad! You're on in a few minutes!

TOMJON LIMPS OFF. HWEL TURNS TO FIND THE WITCHES STARING AT HIM.

HWEL: What are you hanging around here for? Get out there and *curse* them!

HWEL HUSTLES THE WITCHES TOWARDS THE STAGE.

5. CASTLE COURTYARD. EVENING.

THE PLAYER WITCHES ARE ON STAGE ROUND THEIR CAULDRON. NANNY O. AND GRANNY W. ARE WATCHING.

WITCH 3: Sister, where art thou?

WITCH 1: A sailor's wife had chestnuts in her lap and munched and munched and munched.

GRANNY W.: That's us! Round that silly cauldron. That's meant to be us, Gytha.

WITCH 1: Where hast thou been, sister?

WITCH 2: Ha Ha! Killing babes.

NANNY O.: Did you hear that? One of them said we put babbies in the cauldron! They've done a slander on us!

GRANNY W.: Words. That's all that's left. Words. But the words won't be forgotten. They've got a power to them.

WITCH 1: Her husband's to the Rim hath gone, master o' th' Tiger.
But in a sieve I'll thither sail,
And like a rat without a tail,
I'll do and I'll do and I'll do.

WITCH 2: I'll give thee a wind.

WITCH 1: Thou art kind.

WITCH 3: And I another.

WITCH 1: I myself have all the other.

THE AUDIENCE HAS BEGUN TO GET RESTLESS. THEY ARE LOOKING AT NANNY O. AND GRANNY W., MUTTERING AND POINTING AT THEM.

6. GATEHOUSE TOWER. EVENING.

THE STAGE CAN BE SEEN THROUGH A WINDOW IN THE TOWER. MAGRAT IS WATCHING THE PLAY, THE FOOL IS MORE INTERESTED IN MAGRAT.

WITCH 1: And the very ports they blow,
All the quarters that they know
I' th' shipman's card.

MAGRAT: Green blusher? I don't look like that do I?

FOOL: Absolutely not.

MAGRAT: And the hair!

THE FOOL LOOKS AWAY FROM MAGRAT AND OUT OF THE WINDOW AT THE THREE PLAYER WITCHES.

FOOL: Looks like straw. Not very clean either. Not like yours...

MAGRAT HAS LEFT THE TOWER IN SEARCH OF HER COLLEAGUES. THE FOOL TURNS BACK TO FIND HER GONE.

FOOL: Oh. You've gone.

7. BACKSTAGE. EVENING.

TOMJON IS SEARCHING THROUGH THE PROPS BASKET FOR A SUITABLE CROWN.

TOMJON: There's got to be a crown... oh.

HE FINALLY PULLS OUT THE CROWN.

TOMJON: Oh well. You'll have to do.

HE PUTS THE CROWN ON HIS HEAD. HWEL RUNS ACROSS TO TOMJON.

HWEL: You're on!

TOMJON: What...?

WITCH 3: (O.O.S.) A drum! A drum! The king doth...

8. CASTLE COURTYARD. EVENING.

WITCH 3: Ahem. A drum, a drum. The king doth come.

TOMJON (AS THE EVIL KING) ENTERS.

TOMJON: How now, you secret black and mid-night hags, what is't you do?

WITCH 1: A deed without a name.

TOMJON: Such deeds indeed have I performed upon thy saying.

Babes have I slain, their mother's houses burned,

Their father's eyes put out and ears with brands have burned.

It will have blood they say. Blood will have blood,

And fiery is my thirst for blood;

For hearts from chests to pluck and roast upon a spit.

I am in blood stepp'd in so far that,

Should I wade no more,

Returning were as tedious as go o'er.

VERENCE: That's him, isn't it? That's my son.

GRANNY W.: I think he's meant to be you.

VERENCE: I never walked like that! What's happened to his leg... That's my crown he's wearing!

ON STAGE, THE CURTAINS ARE DRAWN TO END ACT ONE.

GRANNY W.: Come, Gytha.

THEY GET UP AND BEGIN TO MAKE THEIR WAY THROUGH THE AUDIENCE, WHO BY NOW ARE BECOMING QUITE THREATENING. AS THEY GO, THEY ARE MET BY MAGRAT.

MAN IN THE CROWD: Murdering old crones—

OTHER MAN: Go and boil your heads in your cauldron! On your broomstick you old hag. Go on out of it.

THE WITCHES PROGRESS THROUGH THE CROWD. THEY ARE WATCHED BY LADY FELMET AND DUKE FELMET.

DUKE FELMET: You must admit, my treasure, the experiment seems to be working.

LADY FELMET: It would appear so.

AS THE WITCHES PROCEED, DEATH RISES AND FOLLOWS THEM.

9. BACKSTAGE. EVENING.

DAFE, WHO HAS BEEN GIVEN THE PART OF DEATH, IS GOING OVER HIS LINES WITH HWEL. HWEL IS ALSO WATCHING A COUPLE OF APPRENTICE ACTORS STRUGGLING WITH A LARGE PIECE OF SCENERY.

DAFE: Cower now, brief mortals! For I am Death, gainst whom no... no...

HWEL: Oh good grief, Dafe! 'Gainst who no lock will hold nor fastened portal bar!'

HWEL NOTICES THAT THE FLAT IS UPSIDE DOWN.

HWEL: Not that way up, you idiots!

DAFE: Right. Gainst whom no... tumty-tum, nor tumty tumty bar.

TOMJON ENTERS FROM THE STAGE. HE CROSSES TO DAFE.

TOMJON: Try a bit more hollowness. Like this.

AS HE SPEAKS, THE VOICE THAT EMERGES FROM HIS LARYNX IS THAT OF DEATH.

TOMJON/DEATH: I have come to get you, you terrible actor!

DAFE: I don't know how you do it. I'll never be as good as you.

DAFE WANDERS IN THE GENERAL DIRECTION OF THE STAGE, STILL PRACTISING HIS LINES.

DAFE: Cower now brief mortals, for I am Death gainst whom no... no... Erm.

THE REAL DEATH WALKS PAST TOMJON, BEHIND HIM. TOMJON LOOKS UNEASY.

10. CASTLE COURTYARD. EVENING.

DUKE FELMET IS HAPPY THAT HIS PLAN SEEMS TO BE WORKING. HE BECKONS A FOOTMAN OVER.

DUKE FELMET: Call the captain of the guard and tell him to find the witches and arrest them. Ha Ha Ha Ha.

11. BACKSTAGE. EVENING.

HWEL AND THE SCENE-SHIFTERS ARE HARD AT WORK. GRANNY W., NANNY O. AND MAGRAT APPEAR. GRANNY W. HAS FOUND A COPY OF THE SCRIPT.

GRANNY W.: 'Divers alarums and excursions'?

MAGRAT: That means lots of terrible happenings.

NANNY O.: Alarums and what?

MAGRAT: Excursions.

NANNY O.: Oh... The seaside would be nice.

MAGRAT: We can't let this happen. Witches just aren't like that. We live in harmony with the great cycles of nature, and do no harm to anyone, and it's wicked of them to say we don't. We ought to fill their bones with hot lead!

GRANNY W.: I don't think that would be appropriate. It could give people the wrong idea.

NANNY O.: But not for long.

MAGRAT: Why don't we just change the words? When they come back on stage we could just put the fluence on them so they forget what they're saying and give them some new words.

GRANNY W.: They'd have to be the proper sort, otherwise people would suspect.

NANNY O.: Shouldn't be too difficult. You just go tumty tumty tumty. Anyway, half of them are forgetting their lines as it is. It'll be easy.

GRANNY W.: All right. I suppose it's worth a try.

12. Backstage. Evening.

ON THE OTHER SIDE OF THE STAGE, THE THREE PLAYER WITCHES ARE SURROUNDED BY A POSSE OF GUARDS, LED BY THE CAPTAIN.

WITCH 2: We're not *really* witches...

CAPTAIN: Tie their hands, lads.

WITCH 3: But if you'd just *listen*, we're with the theatre.

GUARD: Shall we gag them as well, Captain?

THE CAPTAIN NODS.

CAPTAIN: And clap them in chains.

13. Backstage. Evening.

THE ACTORS FOR THE START OF ACT TWO ARE READY TO MAKE THEIR ENTRANCE.

HWEL: The witches! Where are the...?

HE SPOTS MAGRAT, NANNY O. AND GRANNY W. AND BEGINS TO HUSTLE THEM TOWARDS THE STAGE.

HWEL: At last! What are you three playing at? We've been looking for you everywhere!

MAGRAT: Us? But we're not in...

HWEL: Yes you are, remember? We put you in last week.

HWEL SLAPS MAGRAT ON THE BOTTOM.

MAGRAT: Ow!

HWEL: I must say you look as nasty a bunch of hags as a body might hope to clap their eyes on. Run along. Curtain up in ten seconds. Break a leg.

THE WITCHES ALLOW THEMSELVES TO BE SHEPHERDED OUT ONTO THE STAGE.

NANNY O.: Break your own leg.

THEY TAKE THEIR PLACE AROUND THE CAULDRON. GRANNY W. LOOKS UP AT THE LIGHTS AND SMILES GRIMLY.

GRANNY W.: Let's do the show right here.

14. Castle Courtyard. Evening.

THE CURTAINS PART TO ANNOUNCE ACT TWO. THE WITCHES STAND AROUND THEIR CAULDRON, UPSTAGE. DOWNSTAGE, TOMJON LIMPS OUT TO FACE THE AUDIENCE.

TOMJON: What man dare, I dare.

> Approach thou like the rugged Klatchian bear
>
> The arm'd rhinoceros or th' Rham Niz tiger
>
> And I will fear thee not. For now our domination is complete!

NANNY O. GIVES THE CAULDRON A DISMISSIVE KICK.

NANNY O.: It's just a tin one, this.

SHE LOOKS INSIDE.

NANNY O.: And it's full of yuk.

MAGRAT: And the fire is just red paper. Look, you can poke it...

WILMSLOE AND GUMRIDGE ENTER AS THE GOOD DUKE AND HIS LADY. WILMSLOE STARTS HIS LINE, BUT NOTICES THE WITCHES WHICH DRAWS HIM UP SHORT.

NANNY O.: I wouldn't be seen dead with a cauldron like this! Two days' work with a scourer and a bucket of sand is this.

WILMSLOE: The very soil cries out at tyranny... Er.

TOMJON TRIES TO PROMPT WILMSLOE.

TOMJON: And calls me forth for vengeance!

MAGRAT: How do they make it flicker?

GRANNY W.: Be quiet, you two. You're upsetting people. Go ahead, young man. Don't mind us.

TOMJON: Aha! It calls you forth for vengeance, does it? And the heavens cry revenge too, I expect.

THE THREE WITCHES ARE REVEALED TO THE AUDIENCE FOR THE FIRST TIME, IN A SPOTLIGHT. DUKE FELMET IS LOOKING AGHAST.

DUKE FELMET: It's them! What are they doing in my play?

AN ACTOR SOLDIER SIDLES OUT FROM THE WINGS TOWARDS TOMJON.

TOMJON: Aha! Thou callest me an evil king, though thou whisperest it so that none save I might hear it.

THE SOLDIER HISSES AT TOMJON.

SOLDIER: Hwel says what's going on?

TOMJON: What was that? Did I hear you say I come my lord?

SOLDIER: Get these people off, he says.

TOMJON: Thou babblest, man. See how I dodge thy tortoise spear... I said see how I dodge thy tortoise spear!

GRANNY W.: Ghosts of the mind and all device away. I bid the Truth to have its... tumty-tumty... day!

GUMRIDGE: Do you fear him now? And he so mazed with drink?

GUMRIDGE TAKES THE PART OF LADY FELMET. HE HOLDS OUT A DAGGER TO WILMSLOE.

GUMRIDGE: Take this dagger, husband – you are a blade's width from the kingdom.

WILMSLOE TAKES ON THE ROLE OF DUKE FELMET.

WILMSLOE: I dare not.

HWEL THROWS HIS SCRIPT ON THE FLOOR.

HWEL: Ugh!

GUMRIDGE: Who will know? See, there is only eyeless night. Take the dagger now, take the kingdom tomorrow. Have a stab at it, man.

15. Backstage. Evening.

DAFE PREPARES HIMSELF FOR HIS ENTRANCE.

DAFE: Cower now brief mortals. I am Death, Gainst who... Gainst who...

DEATH: (O.O.S.) Whom.

DEATH STEPS OUT OF THE SHADOWS AND STANDS BEHIND HIM.

DAFE: Oh thank you. Gainst whom no lock may hold...

DEATH: Will hold.

DAFE: Oh Gods. It's only three lines! Hwel will... have... my... guts.

DEATH PASSES HIS HAND IN FRONT OF DAFE'S EYES.

DEATH: Forget.

DAFE COLLAPSES.

16. Castle Courtyard. Evening.

THE PLAY, AS DIRECTED BY GRANNY WEATHERWAX, IS CONTINUING.

WILMSLOE: Is this a dagger I see before me?

GUMRIDGE: Of course it's a dagger. Come on. Do it now. The weak deserve no mercy. We'll say he fell down the stairs.

WILMSLOE: I cannot! He has been kindness itself to me!

GUMRIDGE: And you can be Death itself to him!

DEATH MAKES HIS ENTRANCE.

DEATH: Cower now, brief mortals, for I am death, gainst whom no... no... gainst whom... No.

TOMJON PROMPTS HIM.

TOMJON: Lock will hold...

DEATH: What?

TOMJON: Lock will hold nor fastened portal...

DEATH: Lock will hold nor fastened portal... erm...

TOMJON: Bar!

DEATH: Bar.

WILMSLOE: No. No. I cannot do it. Down there in the hall, someone watches.

GUMRIDGE: Dithering idiot! Must I put it in for you? See? His foot is upon the top stair!

DUKE FELMET: (O.O.S.) *No!!!* No!! It wasn't like that!

HE CLIMBS UP ONTO THE STAGE.

DUKE FELMET: You cannot say it was like that! You weren't there!

THE GHOST OF VERENCE STEPS OUT OF THE WINGS AND MERGES WITH THE BODY OF TOMJON. THE VOICE OF VERENCE ISSUES OUT OF TOMJON'S MOUTH.

VERENCE: You traitor! I know it was you! I saw you at the top of the stairs sucking your thumb! I'd kill you now but for the thought of having to spend eternity listening to your whining. I, Verence, formerly king of...

LADY FELMET IS HELPED ONTO THE STAGE. VERENCE IS LEAVING TOMJON'S BODY. THE DUCHESS LOOKS AT HER GUARDS AND THEN POINTS AT THE WITCHES.

LADY FELMET: Arrest them!

THE GUARDS BEGIN TO MAKE THEIR WAY TOWARDS THE WITCHES. A SHOUT FROM THE COURTYARD STOPS THEM.

FOOL: *(O.O.S.)* No!

LADY FELMET: *What* did you say?

THE FOOL ADVANCES TOWARDS THE STAGE.

FOOL: I saw it all. I was in the Great Hall that night. You killed the king, my lord.

DUKE FELMET: I did not. You were not there! I did not see you there! I order you not to be there! You swore loyalty unto death.

FOOL: Yes, my lord. I'm sorry.

THE DUKE WHIPS THE DAGGER OUT OF WILMSLOE'S HAND. HE SCREAMS AT THE FOOL.

DUKE FELMET: You're dead!! Ugh!

HE LUNGES AT THE FOOL AND STABS HIM. THE FOOL SINKS DOWN TO HIS KNEES. MAGRAT RUNS OVER TO HIM AND CRADLES HIS HEAD IN HER BOSOM. THE FOOL FLINGS AWAY HIS CAP OF BELLS.

FOOL: Thank goodness. It's all over.

DUKE FELMET: I didn't do it. You all saw that I didn't do it. You're all lying. Telling lies is naughty.

HE LOOKS AT LADY FELMET.

DUKE FELMET: It was her! She did it!

HE STABS HER TWICE, THEN A COUPLE OF THE ACTORS AND FINALLY HIMSELF.

LADY FELMET: Ugh!

DUKE FELMET: Hahahaha. Ugh! You can't get me now.

HE DROPS THE DAGGER AND LEAVES THE STAGE. GRANNY W. PICKS IT UP AND PUSHES THE BLADE BACK INTO THE HILT.

FOOL: I've never looked a bosom squarely in the face before. Oh cruel world, to save the experience until after I was dead.

MAGRAT: Are you dead?

FOOL: I must be. I think I'm in paradise.

MAGRAT: I think you're alive.

GRANNY W. DEMONSTRATES THE TRICK KNIFE.

GRANNY W.: Everyone's alive. Look. It's a trick dagger. Actors probably can't be trusted with real ones.

NANNY O.: That's right, they can't even keep a cauldron clean.

LADY FELMET: Whether everyone is alive or not is a matter for me to decide. Clearly my husband has lost his wits. And now I decree...

GRANNY W.: Be silent, woman! The true king of Lancre stands before you!

SHE MOTIONS TO TOMJON.

TOMJON: Who? Me?!?

LADY FELMET: Ridiculous. He's a mummer of sorts.

GRANNY W.: He's the true king. We can prove it.

LADY FELMET: Oh no. We're not having that. There'll be no mysterious returned heirs in this kingdom. Guards – take him!

THE GUARDS TAKE A COUPLE OF STEPS TOWARDS TOMJON BEFORE A GESTURE FROM GRANNY W. STOPS THEM.

GUARD 1: She's a witch, isn't she?

LADY FELMET: Certainly.

GUARD 2: We seen where they turn people into newts.

GUARD 1: And then shipwreck them.

LADY FELMET GRABS A SPEAR FROM THE NEAREST GUARD.

LADY FELMET: I'll show you the power of these witches! Ugh!

SHE HURLS IT TOWARDS GRANNY W., WHO CATCHES IT IN MID-FLIGHT. SHE STABS IT INTO THE FLOOR OF THE STAGE.

GRANNY W.: So. It comes to this, does it?

LADY FELMET: Ha Ha.

> GRANNY W. RAISES A FINGER AND POINTS AT HER.
> LADY FELMET LOOKS TERRIFIED AND CRIES OUT.

MAGRAT: What have you done to her?

GRANNY W.: Headology. No-one becomes like she is without building walls inside their head. I've just knocked them down. Everyone wants to know their true self. Now she does.

> LADY FELMET RECOVERS.

LADY FELMET: Guards! I told you to take them!

GRANNY W.: What? But... but I just showed you your true self!

LADY FELMET: I'm supposed to be upset by that, am I? I've seen exactly what I am and I'm proud of it! I'd do it all again, only hotter and longer! I enjoyed it! I did it because I wanted to.

> SHE LOOKS ROUND THE ASSEMBLED COMPANY.

LADY FELMET: There's not one of you who doesn't fear me!

> NANNY O. KNOCKS HER OUT WITH THE CAULDRON.

NANNY O.: She does go on, doesn't she.

GRANNY W.: Take her away and put her in a cell somewhere.

> THE GUARDS STRUGGLE TO REMOVE LADY FELMET.
> GRANNY W. LOOKS AT TOMJON.

GRANNY W.: Now my lad. You're the new king of Lancre.

TOMJON: But I don't know how to be king!

GRANNY W.: We all seed you. You had it down just right, including the shouting.

TOMJON: But that's just acting!

GRANNY W.: Well act then.

17. LANCRE CASTLE. CORRIDOR. NIGHT.

> DUKE FELMET IS PRETENDING TO BE A GHOST. DEATH
> IS WALKING ALONG BESIDE HIM, POINTING TO AN
> HOUR-GLASS.

DUKE FELMET: Whooooo! Whooooo!

DEATH: But I assure you, you are not dead. Take it from me.

> DUKE FELMET REMOVES THE SHEET FROM HIS HEAD.

DUKE FELMET: Hahahaha. I shall rattle my bones at night and knock on tables and drip ectoplasm on anyone I don't like. Hahahaha.

DEATH: It won't work. Living people aren't allowed to be ghosts.

> DUKE FELMET REPLACES HIS SHEET AND WALKS
> TOWARDS A WALL.

DUKE FELMET: I'm going to float through walls.

> HE BANGS INTO IT RATHER HEAVILY.

DUKE FELMET: Ow.

DEATH: I give up.

18. LANCRE CASTLE. THE DUNGEONS. NIGHT.

> LADY FELMET IS BEING DRAGGED TOWARDS A CELL
> BY THE GUARDS. THEY PASS ANOTHER CELL. THE
> THREE PLAYER WITCHES RUSH TO THE BARS TO
> PROTEST THEIR INNOCENCE.

WITCH 1: I say? There's been some laughable mistake. Look, the wigs come right off...

> THEY DEMONSTRATE. THE GUARDS PAY NO
> ATTENTION.

19. LANCRE CASTLE. THRONE ROOM. NIGHT.

> THE DIGNITARIES OF LANCRE HAVE MOVED TO THE
> THRONE ROOM. TOMJON IS SITTING UNHAPPILY ON
> THE THRONE. HWEL SITS BESIDE THE THRONE,
> WORKING ON HIS NEW OPUS 'THE KING OF LANCRE'.
> GRANNY W. STANDS ON THE OTHER SIDE.

TOMJON: I don't want to be king!

GRANNY W.: (V.O.) Let him be whoever he thinks he is—

TOMJON: Everyone says I take after my dad!

HWEL: Funny thing, all this taking after people. I mean, if I took after my dad, I'd be a hundred feet underground digging rocks.

TOMJON: Besides, I've got to get back. There's Chrysophase. If we don't get the money to him in time, he'll come looking for us.

HWEL: Eh?

TOMJON: An arm and a leg, remember?

GRANNY W.: It might be a good idea to hold the coronation tomorrow. It's not good for a kingdom to be without a ruler. It doesn't like it.

TOMJON: I told you. I don't want to be king!

MAGRAT, NANNY O. AND THE FOOL ARE AT THE FAR END OF THE ROOM. MAGRAT IS WHISPERING TO NANNY O.

MAGRAT: You were right. They really are brothers aren't they?

NANNY O.: Oh yes. Definitely. I saw to his mother when your *(SHE POINTS TO THE FOOL)* – when he was born. And to the queen when young Tomjon was born, and Her Majesty told me who his father was.

MAGRAT: But Verence was her husband, wasn't he. So... and so... and... oh!

NANNY O.: You know what they say. Fools rush in when the king's away. Or something like that.

THE TRIO ARRIVE THROUGH THE CROWD AT THE THRONE. THE FOOL LOOKS AT TOMJON. NOW THE FOOL HAS REMOVED HIS CAP OF BELLS, THEY DO LOOK REMARKABLY SIMILAR.

NANNY O.: But we'll keep that to ourselves, eh?

20. LANCRE CASTLE. THE RAMPARTS. NIGHT.

DUKE FELMET IS STILL TRYING TO HAUNT THE CASTLE. DEATH IS STILL TRYING TO PERSUADE HIM THAT HE ISN'T A GHOST.

DUKE FELMET: Well then, if I'm not a ghost, why are you here?

DEATH: Waiting.

THE DUKE LEAPS UP ON TO THE RAMPART WALLS.

DUKE FELMET: Wait forever, bone face. I shall hover in the twilight world, I shall find some chains to shake, I shall...

HE MISSES HIS FOOTING AND PLUNGES INTO THE ABYSS BENEATH THE CASTLE WALLS.

DUKE FELMET: I shall haunt their corridors and whisper under their doors on still nights.

DEATH: Now you're talking.

21. LANCRE CASTLE. GREAT HALL. EVENING/NIGHT.

THE CORONATION OF KING VERENCE II REX HAS TAKEN PLACE. THE DIGNITARIES OF LANCRE, THEIR LADY WIVES, AMBASSADORS FROM NEARBY KINGDOMS, NOT TO MENTION NANNY O. AND GRANNY W., ARE ENJOYING A GREAT FEAST.

LADY FELMET EMERGES AND MAKES HER WAY TOWARDS THE PINE FOREST.

LADY FELMET: I'll be back. And I won't burden myself with a husband next time, either. Weak. No courage in him to be as bad as he knew he was inside...

SHE CARRIES ON THROUGH THE FOREST. IT BECOMES MORE DENSE. THE BRANCHES TEAR AT HER CLOTHES AND HAIR. THE PATH HAS BECOME TOO DENSELY OVERGROWN FOR HER TO CONTINUE. A CLIFF FACE CONFRONTS HER. SHE STOPS AND TURNS.

THE PATH SHE HAS TAKEN IS BEING OBLITERATED AS THE TREES MOVE ACROSS IT. CREEPERS SNAKE DOWN FROM THE PINES.

A CREEPER SNAKES AROUND HER NECK. THE FOREST CLOSES IN ON HER.

LADY FELMET: Noooooooo!

DUKE FELMET: *(V.O.)* Hahahahahaha.

22. MOOR BY THE STANDING STONE. NIGHT.

THE THREE WITCHES HAVE GATHERED.

GRANNY W.: It was a good banquet, I thought.

NANNY O.: Yes, I was nearly sick! And my Shirl helped out in the kitchen and brought me home some scraps.

GRANNY W.: I heard half a pig and three bottles of fizzy wine went missing they say. We were a bit surprised you weren't there, Magrat.

NANNY O.: We thought you'd be up at the top of the table, kind of thing.

MAGRAT: I wasn't invited.

GRANNY W.: Well, I don't know about *invited*. We weren't *invited*. People don't invite witches. They just know we'll turn up if we want to.

MAGRAT: Well, he's been very busy, sorting everything out, you know.

GRANNY W.: I daresay he'll get around to everything, sooner or later. It's very demanding being a king.

MAGRAT: Yes.

GRANNY W.: Here. Your hair looks a bit grubby. Have you washed it lately?

MAGRAT BURSTS INTO TEARS.

23. ANKH-MORPORK. THE DYSK THEATRE. NIGHT.

THE AUDIENCE APPLAUD AS TOMJON TAKES HIS BOW AT THE END OF A PERFORMANCE BY VITOLLER'S PLAYERS.

TOMJON COMES INTO THE WINGS. HE IS GREETED BY VITOLLER. HWEL IS OVERSEEING THE PROCEEDINGS.

VITOLLER: Well laddie, you did it again!

TOMJON: I know.

HE TURNS TO HWEL.

TOMJON: How's the play going?

HWEL: Hmmn? What play?

TOMJON: You know. That one. The Lancre King.

HWEL: Oh, coming along. I'll get round to finishing it one of these days.

24. MAGRAT'S COTTAGE. DAY.

THE FOOL AND A SERGEANT HAVE ARRIVED ON HORSEBACK. THE FOOL IS DRESSED AS A KING. THE SERGEANT APPROACHES MAGRAT'S DOOR.

THE SERGEANT KNOCKS.

SERGEANT: *Open in the name of the King!*

FOOL: Alright! You don't have to shout like that.

SERGEANT: Sorry sire.

FOOL: Try the latch.

SERGEANT: Don't like the sound of that, sire. Could be dangerous. If you want my advice, sire, I'd set fire to the thatch.

FOOL: Set fire? I don't think that would be appropriate, Sergeant. I think I'll try the latch, if it's all the same to you.

SERGEANT: Well couldn't I just set fire to the privy?

FOOL: Absolutely not!

SERGEANT: That chicken house over there looks as if it would go up like...

FOOL: Sergeant! Go back to the castle.

SERGEANT: What? And leave you all alone, sire?

FOOL: There are times when even a king needs to be alone.

SERGEANT: Sire?

FOOL: It concerns a Lady.

SERGEANT: Ah. Point taken sire.

HE GOES BACK TO HIS HORSE AND REMOUNTS.

SERGEANT: If you have any trouble getting her alight you know where I live.

THE FOOL RAISES HIS HAND TO KNOCK AT THE DOOR. BUT BEFORE HE CAN DO SO, IT IS OPENED. MAGRAT STANDS INSIDE THE COTTAGE. THEY LOOK AT ONE ANOTHER FOR A MOMENT. THE FOOL ENTERS. THE DOOR CLOSES AGAIN.

THE END